Mary Sue Taylor

Prayer for Daybreak and Day's End

VOLUME II

July Through December

ST.
ANTHONY
MESSENGER
PRESS

CINCINNATI, OHIO

In gratitude to

Father Inocencio Estibalez
and
Father Edward Lamp

for their spiritual direction
and inspiration

Nihil Obstat: Rev. Thomas Richstatter, O.F.M.
Rev. Robert L. Hagedorn

Imprimi Potest: Rev. John Bok, O.F.M.
Provincial

Imprimatur: Rev. R. Daniel Conlon, V.G.
Archdiocese of Cincinnati
July 19, 1993

Scripture citations are taken from *The New American Bible With Revised New Testament*, copyright ©1986 by the Confraternity of Christian Doctrine, and are used by permission. All rights reserved.

Cover and book design by Julie Lonneman
Illustrations by Paula Wiggins

ISBN 0-86716-148-5

Published by St. Anthony Messenger Press
Printed in the U.S.A.

Introduction

Rising early, you stumble, still sleepy-eyed, to your place of prayer. At day's end, you refuse the welcoming bed while you weave the day's loose ends into your prayer. Such moments put you in community with the priests, religious and laity all over the world who celebrate common prayer at fixed intervals throughout the day.

The Liturgy of the Hours (also referred to as the Divine Office or the Breviary) has its origins in Christ himself, who enjoined us to "pray unceasingly." From the times of the early Church, believers have gathered at specified times, day and night, to pray and praise God. United in prayer, the community of the faithful lifts its collective voice in psalmody and joins with Christ and the Church in a prayer for all of humankind—especially at the "hinges" of the day, morning and evening.

This easy-to-use book of Morning and Evening Prayers borrows from the tradition. While the Liturgy of the Hours is a voluminous, complex and costly four-volume set, this two-volume set offers a simplified, concise format. It is arranged by date. Volume One begins with New Year's Day and ends with June 30; Volume Two will take you from July 1 to December 31. All you need to do is turn to the day's date. The Canticles, one of which closes each prayer session, are printed on a separate card that will serve as your bookmark.

The Components of Morning Prayer

Morning Prayer begins with a salutation and continues with a selection from Psalms. These Opening Songs are used for an entire week. (The fourth "week" of each month has more than seven days.)

Scripture Reading: Most of the Scripture selections follow the Church's liturgical calendar; others relate to the season or to a particular theme. Scripture passages are kept short purposely. You are invited to read the surrounding text in your own Bible, so that the meaning is understood in its proper context.

Because dates for Lent and Easter Season vary each year, this calendar-based book does not include prayer for specific seasonal days (Ash Wednesday, Good Friday, etc.). Prayers for February and March, however, follow a Lenten theme while prayers for April focus on the Resurrection.

Putting Prayer Into Practive gives suggestions for integrating the Scripture into daily life. *Words of Wisdom* come from a spiritual master, usually a saint, pope or theologian. A *Meditation* or *Spiritual Exercise* is a discipline to expand and deepen the soul's prayer journey. Only one of these techniques is used each day; they are presented alternately throughout the book.

Prayer: A gentle prayer-poem builds on the Scripture theme and sets the mood for carrying spiritual values into the day's work and play.

Canticle: One of the beautiful word-songs attributed to saints and biblical figures and found on the bookmark.

The Components of Evening Prayer

Evening Prayer begins with a salutation and continues with a selection from Psalms. These Opening Songs are used for an entire week. (The fourth "week" of each month has more than seven days.)

Scripture Reading: The Scripture selection for Evening

Prayer is usually the same as for Morning Prayer.

Reflection: A few questions upon which to reflect, based on the Scripture theme and the practical suggestions for applying the Scripture theme to daily life. Suggestions for keeping a spiritual journal are given occasionally.

Prayer: A brief prayer of thanksgiving or praise.

Canticle: Another of the word-songs found on the bookmark.

Overall, this book attempts to present a prayer expression geared for the spirituality of the 1990's and beyond. May it enrich your prayer life!

July

Opening Song for Morning Prayer

SALUTATION

Awake! You are made for joy and praise and singing. You are God's work of art.

SONG Psalm 8:2-7a

O LORD, our Lord,
    how glorious is your name over all the earth!
    You have exalted your majesty above the heavens.
Out of the mouths of babes and sucklings
    you have fashioned praise because of your foes,
    to silence the hostile and the vengeful.
When I behold your heavens, the work of your fingers,
    the moon and stars which you set in place—
What is man that you should be mindful of him,
    or the son of man that you should care for him?

You have made him little less than the angels
    and crowned him with glory and honor.
You have given him rule over the works of your hands....

Turn to the page with today's date for the continuation of Morning Prayer.

Opening Song for Evening Prayer

SALUTATION

In this week of festivals and fireworks,
sound and light,
we salute you, Divine Creator,
and acknowledge your precious gift of free will.

SONG

Only we, of all creatures, have the choice
  to sing the song of the Earth,
to join in the dance of life
  and move in the established harmony
  of the rest of creation.
We hear the universe in our being
  as the universe gathers us in its being.[1]

Turn to the page with today's date for the continuation of
Evening Prayer.

Morning Prayer

Begin with page 6.

SCRIPTURE Amos 3:9b-11

> "Gather about the mountains of Samaria,
>   and see the great disorders within her,
>   the oppression in her midst."
> For they know not how to do what is right,
>   says the LORD,
> Storing up in their castles
>   what they have extorted and robbed.
>   Therefore, thus says the Lord GOD:
> An enemy shall surround the land,
>   and strip you of your strength,
>   and pillage your castles.

WORDS OF WISDOM

(This month of July, with its emphasis on independence and freedom, seems an appropriate time to reflect on words from various social justice encyclicals.)

It is shameful and inhuman...to use men as things for gain and to put no more value on them than what they are worth in muscle and energy.... Among the most important duties of employers the principal one is to give every worker what is justly due him....

Workers' associations ought to be so constituted and so governed as to furnish the most suitable and most convenient means to attain the object proposed...: that the individual members...secure, so far as possible, an

increase in the goods of body, of soul, and of prosperity.
(Leo XIII)[2]

PRAYER

God, give us the grace to share.
Let no one possess the land,
for it is in the attitude of possession
that abuse occurs.

CANTICLE Canticle of St. Francis

Evening Prayer

Begin with page 7.

SCRIPTURE *See page 8.*

REFLECTION

What kind of power do I have, as an individual, to bring
about a more just world?

PRAYER

In fairness, Lord God,
you create and govern the land.
Glory be to your name!

CANTICLE Canticle of Judith

Morning Prayer

Begin with page 6.

SCRIPTURE Psalm 73:7-11

> Out of their crassness comes iniquity;
>   their fancies overflow their hearts.
> They scoff and speak evil;
>   outrage from on high they threaten.
> They set their mouthings in place of heaven,
>   and their pronouncements roam the earth.
> "So he brings his people to such a pass
>   that they have not even water!"
> And they say, "How does God know?"
>   And, "Is there any knowledge in the Most High?"

WORDS OF WISDOM

...[T]win rocks of shipwreck must be carefully avoided. For, as one is wrecked upon, or comes close to, what is known as individualism by denying or minimizing the social and public character of the right of property, so by rejecting or minimizing the private and individual character of this same right, one inevitably runs into collectivism or at least closely approaches its tenets....

Free competition has destroyed itself; economic dictatorship has supplanted the free market; unbridled ambition for power has likewise succeeded greed for gain; all economic life has become tragically hard, inexorable, and cruel. (Pius XI)[3]

PRAYER

We are your hands, Lord.
Help us build a just society where the well-being
of employer and employee, worker and owner,
may be honored.

CANTICLE Wisdom Canticle

Evening Prayer

Begin with page 7.

SCRIPTURE *See page 10.*

REFLECTION

What unfairness do I see in the economic system?

PRAYER

Original Owner,
you share and serve your creation.
May we, too, follow your model
as we assume ownership
of your earthly kingdom.
Bless us
and make us worthy stewards
of your creation.

CANTICLE Canticle of St. Francis

Morning Prayer

Begin with page 6.

SCRIPTURE Genesis 3:22-24

Then, the LORD God said, "See! the man has become like
one of us, knowing what is good and what is bad!
Therefore, he must not be allowed to put out his hand
and take fruit from the tree of life also, and thus eat of it
and live forever." The LORD God therefore banished him
from the garden of Eden, to till the ground from which
he had been taken. When he expelled the man, he
settled him east of the garden of Eden; and he stationed
the cherubim and the fiery revolving sword, to guard the
way to the tree of life.

WORDS OF WISDOM

A great religious persecution broke out in the land and
the three Pillars of religion, Scripture, Worship and
Charity, appeared before God to express their fear that,
if religion was stamped out, they would cease to exist.

"Not to worry," said the Lord. "I plan to send One to
earth who is greater than all of you."

"By what name is this Great One called?"

"Self-knowledge," said God. "He will do greater things
than any of you have done." (Anthony de Mello, S.J.)[4]

PRAYER

Help me, Lord, to love myself enough to speak the truth, to act with integrity and to make peace with the dark and unruly side of my nature. Gently and gracefully, may I today acknowledge and embrace at least one of my weak and vulnerable parts.

CANTICLE Canticle of Judith

Evening Prayer

Begin with page 7.

SCRIPTURE *See page 12.*

REFLECTION

Today did I own up to one feeble trait that I never admitted before? Now that I've admitted it, how am I going to treat it, with patience and understanding or disgust and fear?

PRAYER

Creator God,
I am grateful for the thorn in my flesh.
May the knowledge of this weakness help me
to become humble and forgiving.

Our Father....

CANTICLE Canticle of Mary

Morning Prayer

Begin with page 6.

SCRIPTURE Isaiah 61:1-2

> The Spirit of the Lord GOD is upon me,
>   because the Lord has anointed me;
> He has sent me to bring glad tidings to the lowly,
>   to heal the brokenhearted,
> To proclaim liberty to the captives,
>   and release to the prisoners,
> To announce a year of favor from the LORD
>   and a day of vindication by our God,
>   to comfort all who mourn.

PUTTING PRAYER INTO PRACTICE

Sitting straight, yet relaxed, lead yourself into a quiet meditation on the word *freedom*. Bask in gratitude as you become aware of the freedom you possess. Bask in gratitude also as you become aware of some of the areas where you are not as free as you would like to be. Remember that a problem, once identified, is eventually solved. It is the unidentified bondage in each life that imprisons.

PRAYER

Father/Mother God, I rejoice in my freedoms,
in the knowledge and awareness of problem areas,
places in my life where I am not free,
and at the opportunity to solve these problems.

CANTICLE Canticle of St. Patrick

Evening Prayer

Begin with page 7.

SCRIPTURE *See page 14.*

REFLECTION

Do I take my gifts, freedoms and riches for granted? In what areas of my life am I not free?

PRAYER

The entire day, Lord, has been a celebration of the gifts of the planet earth and our nation's land. Thank you for it all, especially our vision of democracy, liberty and justice.

CANTICLE Canticle of Zechariah

Morning Prayer

Begin with page 6.

SCRIPTURE Luke 7:12-15

As [Jesus] drew near to the gate of the city [Nain], a man who had died was being carried out, the only son of his mother, and she was a widow. A large crowd from the city was with her. When the Lord saw her, he was moved with pity for her and said to her, "Do not weep." He stepped forward and touched the coffin; at this the bearers halted, and he said, "Young man, I tell you, arise!" The dead man sat up and began to speak, and Jesus gave him to his mother.

WORDS OF WISDOM

If I am to perceive God's word within myself, I have to be alienated from all that is mine, especially from the realm of the temporal.... People...who truly know that, even if they give up themselves and everything else, all this is just nothing—ah, people who live *in this way* truly possess all things. (Meister Eckhart)[5]

PRAYER

Creator God,
help me to understand
that the world is not a hostile place,
but a planet in harmony with your divine will.
Give me the grace, God, to see and connect
with the invisible sources of sustenance
with which you surround me.

CANTICLE Canticle of Mary

Evening Prayer

Begin with page 7.

SCRIPTURE *See page 16.*

REFLECTION

Today, did I find myself "dead" or "asleep" to the moment because I was worrying about myself or another? In what ways did guilt or insecurity distract me from being fully alive?

PRAYER

Thank you, Lord,
for giving me each day
people and events
that bring me closer to you.
Help me to be alert
to their lessons.

CANTICLE Wisdom Canticle

Morning Prayer

Begin with page 6.

SCRIPTURE Amos 5:21-24

I hate, I spurn your feasts,
   I take no pleasure in your solemnities;
Your cereal offerings I will not accept,
   nor consider your stall-fed peace offerings.
Away with your noisy songs!
   I will not listen to the melodies of your harps.
But if you would offer me holocausts,
   then let justice surge like water
   and goodness like an unfailing stream.

PUTTING PRAYER INTO PRACTICE

Consumerism is one way you can use your personal
power to effect justice. Did you know that a "driving
force behind the destruction of the tropical rain forests is
the American meat habit"? Trees are cut down to provide
pastureland for cattle. Each year 200,000,000 pounds of
meat are imported from Costa Rica, El Salvador,
Guatemala, Nicaragua, Honduras and Panama while the
average inhabitant of any of these countries consumes
less meat than the average American house cat.[6]

PRAYER

May I find the way, Almighty Liberator,
to live with integrity and promote justice
so that my worship may not be
an empty act or meaningless ritual.

CANTICLE Canticle of St. Patrick

Evening Prayer

Begin with page 7.

SCRIPTURE *See page 18.*

REFLECTION

In what way did my justice flow today?

PRAYER

You restore justice
and maintain equilibrium.
In you, Prince of Peace,
I place my trust.

CANTICLE Canticle of Judith

Morning Prayer

Begin with page 6.

SCRIPTURE Matthew 9:6-7

"But that you may know that the Son of Man has authority on earth to forgive sins"—he then said to the paralytic, "Rise, pick up your stretcher, and go home." He rose and went home.

PUTTING PRAYER INTO PRACTICE

How often are we paralyzed by our sins and fears? Remember your divine origins today when something starts to get you down. Say to yourself, "Arise and walk. Your darkest sins are forgiven you. You are a child of the light."

PRAYER

Awake, alert
and ready to respond,
may I move and act
as a healed being,
free of corruption.

CANTICLE Canticle of Judith

Evening Prayer

Begin with page 7.

SCRIPTURE Matthew 9:6b

Rise, pick up your stretcher, and go home.

REFLECTION

Did I raise myself up today, at least once, out of a state of fear, depression or darkness?

Enter your reflections in your spiritual journal, if you are keeping one.

PRAYER

Into my life you come,
removing the dis-ease
and soothing the pain.
I stand before you
healed and happy.

CANTICLE Canticle of Mary

Opening Song for Morning Prayer

SALUTATION

Awaken, my soul, to the song of the earth,
  To the history of the place—the dream of its Creator
    coming true.
Let yourself sink into the generous stream of life,
Drink of your oneness with all living things
  and be healed
  and be made whole.[7]

SONG

Each creature has its own inner life,
  Its mystery, its sacred quality.
Humans have feared what is different,
  Have demanded conformity and submission.
Let us now choose to join the song of the earth,
  For in us the universe will at last contemplate
And celebrate the differences.[8]

Turn to the page with today's date for the continuation of Morning Prayer.

Opening Song for Evening Prayer

SALUTATION

No longer shall the sun
  be your light by day,
Nor the brightness of the moon
  shine upon you at night;
The LORD shall be your light forever,
  your God shall be your glory. (Isaiah 60:19)

SONG

The earth sings of life's mysteries,
Rhythms of giving and receiving,
Suffering and Joy,
Seasons of Waiting and Fulfillment,
Birth and Death.

The universe has slowly revealed its secrets
  to science—the unfolding story of millenni[a]....
Now the human heart
  can gather up these secrets
and, filled with wonder and delight,
  sing them into praise![9]

Turn to the page with today's date for the continuation of Evening Prayer.

Morning Prayer

Begin with page 22.

SCRIPTURE Matthew 9:12b-13

Those who are well do not need a physician, but the sick
do. Go and learn the meaning of the words, "I desire
mercy, not sacrifice." I did not come to call the righteous
but sinners.

COMMENTARY

If Christ came to call the unhealthy and deliver a
message of mercy, what is our responsibility as Church?
What would happen in your place of worship if a dirty
street person came in to pray? What is the response of
the "pillars of the Church" when a "black sheep" wants to
enter the flock?

PRAYER

In the bowels of iniquity,
in the streets of the slums,
in the horrors of prison,
let me demonstrate your mercy, Lord.
For the people in paradise
have no need or use for it.

CANTICLE Canticle of Zechariah

Evening Prayer

Begin with page 23.

SCRIPTURE *See page 24.*

REFLECTION

How can I, as a member of my worshiping community, make newcomers feel accepted and welcomed— especially those who are not appreciated by society in general?

PRAYER

Merciful Maker,
you came to free me
from bondage to self.
My grateful heart sings for joy.

CANTICLE Canticle of Judith

Morning Prayer

Begin with page 22.

SCRIPTURE Matthew 11:16-19

To what shall I compare this generation? It is like children who sit in marketplaces and call to one another, "We played the flute for you, but you did not dance, we sang a dirge but you did not mourn." For John came neither eating nor drinking, and they said, "He is possessed by a demon." The Son of Man came eating and drinking and they said, "Look, he is a glutton and a drunkard, a friend of tax collectors and sinners." But wisdom is vindicated by her works.

PUTTING PRAYER INTO PRACTICE

Whether you are sorrowful or joyful, focus today on discerning and carrying out the Father's will. If you are in the flow of the divine plan, you will be vindicated by your works.

PRAYER

I will sing you a song,
Maker of all Melodies,
in rhythm with the flow
of your divine Spirit.
Give me the grace
to play well before you,
Lord and Creator!

CANTICLE Canticle of Judith

Evening Prayer

Begin with page 23.

SCRIPTURE *See page 26.*

REFLECTION

Was I in tune with the Spirit today? When?

Enter your reflections in your spiritual journal, if you are keeping one.

PRAYER

As night approaches,
Lord of the Dance,
carry me off in your arms
so that my soul may be refreshed
by the healing harmony of your presence.

CANTICLE Wisdom Canticle

Morning Prayer

Begin with page 22.

SCRIPTURE Matthew 11:25b

I give praise to you, Father, Lord of heaven and earth, for
although you have hidden these things from the wise
and the learned, you have revealed them to the childlike.

PRAYER

Open my eyes, Lord,
to the mysteries and miracles
that surround me daily.
In a child-like attitude,
I seek your instruction
and place myself in your hands,
happy in the knowledge
that your will is unfolding around me.

CANTICLE Canticle of St. Patrick

Evening Prayer

Begin with page 23.

SCRIPTURE *See page 28.*

REFLECTION

What attitudes block my growth?

PRAYER

Brother Jesus,
in tenderness you reach out
and console me.
Even in my sin and separation
you hunt me down
and carry me home.
I rest in your arms.

CANTICLE Canticle of St. Francis

Morning Prayer

Begin with page 22.

SCRIPTURE Matthew 25:35c, 40b

[I was] a stranger and you welcomed me.... Amen, I say to you, whatever you did for one of the least brothers of mine, you did for me.

PUTTING PRAYER INTO PRACTICE

Benedictine monasteries are usually fine examples of Christian hospitality. Laypeople, both men and women, who are serious about their prayer life, are welcome to stay with the monks—to pray, eat and share life with them. For those seeking a monastic experience for a few days or a week, this is an excellent opportunity. The Benedictines somehow manage to maintain the sanctity and awe of a cloister while opening up to all who seek to share their spirituality.

PRAYER

Spirit of Life,
help me find the right balance
between the inner and outer life
so that I can extend,
in the spirit of hospitality,
the gift of peace and nourishment
to my brothers and sisters.

CANTICLE Canticle of Zechariah

Evening Prayer

Begin with page 23.

SCRIPTURE *See page 30.*

REFLECTION

In what ways, today, did I extend Christian hospitality to others?

Enter your reflections in your spiritual journal, if you are keeping one.

PRAYER

Awaken in me, Lord, a spirit of sharing.
Sometimes it is hard for me
to see and acknowledge my gifts.
Rid me of this false humility!
As I grow in gratefulness,
may I grow in generosity.

CANTICLE Canticle of Mary

Morning Prayer

Begin with page 22.

SCRIPTURE John 8:31-35

Jesus then said to the Jews who believed in him, "If you remain in my word, you will truly be my disciples, and you will know the truth, and the truth will set you free." They answered him, "We are descendants of Abraham and have never been enslaved to anyone. How can you say, 'You will become free'?" Jesus answered them, "Amen, amen, I say to you, everyone who commits sin is a slave of sin. A slave does not remain in a household forever, but a son always remains."

PUTTING PRAYER INTO PRACTICE

To be honest with others, you must first be honest with yourself. Today, as you are conversing with others, notice the times you exaggerate, minimize, withhold or distort the truth.

PRAYER

Merciful Father,
lead me to a life of openness, truth and love
so that I can come into my inheritance
as a child of God.
For it is only when I understand your word as my own
that I can claim to be your daughter or son.

CANTICLE Canticle of Zechariah

Evening Prayer

Begin with page 23.

SCRIPTURE *See page 32.*

REFLECTION

Why am I afraid to be me? What steps can I take to begin to move out of this place of fear?

PRAYER

For the gift of free will
and the courage to make the right choice,
I thank you, Lord.

CANTICLE Wisdom Canticle

Morning Prayer

Begin with page 22.

SCRIPTURE Psalm 15:1-3

O Lᴏʀᴅ, who shall sojourn in your tent?
  Who shall dwell on your holy mountain?

He who walks blamelessly and does justice;
  who thinks the truth in his heart
  and slanders not with his tongue;
Who harms not his fellow man,
  nor takes up a reproach against his neighbor....

WORDS OF WISDOM

Perhaps the most pressing question of our day concerns
the relationship between economically advanced
commonwealths and those that are in the process of
development. The former enjoy the conveniences of life;
the latter experience dire poverty.... Mindful of our role
as universal father, we think it opportune to stress here
what we have stated in another connection: "We all share
responsibility for the fact that populations are
undernourished. Therefore it is necessary to arouse a
sense of responsibility in individuals and generally,
especially among those more blessed with this world's
goods." (John XXIII)[10]

PRAYER

> Yahweh, on your mountain
> I long to roam.
> Free me from my selfishness
> so I can reach the heights
> where you dwell.

CANTICLE Canticle of St. Francis

Evening Prayer

Begin with page 23.

SCRIPTURE *See page 34.*

REFLECTION

> Of the six things Yahweh asks of us in Psalm 15, which one am I closest to attaining?

PRAYER

> Source of Life,
> you call us home.
> It is your mercy
> that allows us to return.

CANTICLE Canticle of Judith

Morning Prayer

Begin with page 22.

SCRIPTURE Romans 8:19-21; 26

> For creation awaits with eager expectation the revelation
> of the children of God; for creation was made subject to
> futility, not of its own accord but because of the one who
> subjected it, in hope that creation itself would be set free
> from slavery to corruption and share in the glorious
> freedom of the children of God....
>
> In the same way, the Spirit too comes to the aid of our
> weakness; for we do not know how to pray as we ought,
> but the Spirit itself intercedes with inexpressible
> groanings.

WORDS OF WISDOM

> To be alive is to be addicted and to be alive and addicted
> is to stand in need of grace. Addiction is defined as any
> compulsive habitual behavior (such as worrying,
> watching TV, etc.) that limits the freedom of human
> desire. Although addiction is natural, it severely impedes
> human freedom...and makes us slaves to our
> compulsions. Grace, the freely flowing power of divine
> love, is the only hope for true freedom from this
> enslavement. (Gerald C. May, M.D.)[11]

PRAYER

> Only by your grace, Lord,
> does my soul have wings
> and my spirit soar free.
> Give me the patience and perseverance
> to understand myself and see my addictions.
> Lead me, Lord, one step at a time,
> from compulsive behavior to freedom.

CANTICLE Canticle of Mary

Evening Prayer

Begin with page 23.

SCRIPTURE *See page 36.*

REFLECTION

> Did I identify and acknowledge at least one addiction?

PRAYER

> I groan inwardly,
> stuck in my own doubt and guilt,
> but your forgiveness and grace
> free me.

CANTICLE Canticle of Judith

Opening Song for Morning Prayer

SALUTATION

As the first streaks of light
signal the start of a new day,
my heart awakens to your loving presence,
Lord of Light!

SONG Psalm 1:1-3

Happy the man who follows not
    the counsel of the wicked
Nor walks in the way of sinners,
    nor sits in the company of the insolent,
But delights in the law of the LORD
    and meditates on his law day and night.
He is like a tree
    planted near running water,
That yields its fruit in due season,
    and whose leaves never fade.
    [Whatever he does, prospers.]

Turn to the page with today's date for the continuation of Morning Prayer.

Opening Song for Evening Prayer

SALUTATION

> You will sing
>> as on a night when a feast is observed,
> And be merry of heart
>> as one marching along with a flute
> Toward the mountain of the LORD,
>> toward the Rock of Israel,
>> accompanied by the timbrels and lyres. (Isaiah 30:29)

SONG Isaiah 55:12-13

> Yes, in joy you shall depart,
>> in peace you shall be brought back;
> Mountains and hills shall break out in song before you,
>> and all the trees of the countryside shall clap their
>> hands.
> In place of the thornbush, the cypress shall grow,
>> instead of nettles, the myrtle.
> This shall be to the LORD's renown,
>> an everlasting imperishable sign.

Turn to the page with today's date for the continuation of Evening Prayer.

Morning Prayer

Begin with page 38.

SCRIPTURE Romans 8:22-25

We know that all creation is groaning in labor pains even
until now; and not only that, but we ourselves, who have
the firstfruits of the Spirit, we also groan within
ourselves as we wait for adoption, the redemption of our
bodies. For in hope we were saved. Now hope that sees
for itself is not hope. For who hopes for what one sees?
But if we hope for what we do not see, we wait with
endurance.

COMMENTARY

A groan is a sound of effort, stretching or endurance. It
can also be a sound of pain such as the communal groan
of people who struggle for justice or an individual lament
over loneliness or disease.

PRAYER

In my groaning, God,
I reach out to you in hope
and "wait with
endurance."

CANTICLE Canticle of Zechariah

Evening Prayer

Begin with page 39.

SCRIPTURE *See page 40.*

REFLECTION

In what ways do I groan? What kind of groan do I hear
from others?

PRAYER

You are here, Lord,
even when I try to hide;
you are always ready
to soothe and heal my labor pains.

CANTICLE Canticle of Mary

Morning Prayer

Begin with page 38.

SCRIPTURE Matthew 13:3b-9

A sower went out to sow. And as he sowed, some seed fell on the path, and birds came and ate it up. Some fell on rocky ground, where it had little soil. It sprang at once because the soil was not deep, and when the sun rose it was scorched, and it withered for lack of roots. Some seed fell among thorns, and the thorns grew up and choked it. But some seed fell on rich soil, and produced fruit, a hundred or sixty or thirtyfold. Whoever has ears ought to hear.

STORY

"Ah, there you are! [the bishop] said. "I'm glad to see you. But I gave you the candlesticks, too, which are silver like the rest and would bring two hundred francs. Why didn't you take them along with your cutlery?"

Jean Valjean opened his eyes and looked at the bishop with an expression no human tongue could describe.

"Monseigneur," said the brigadier, "then what this man said is true? We met him. He was acting like a fugitive, and we arrested him in order to find out. He had this silver."

"...And you brought him back here? It's all a mistake."

"If that's so," said the brigadier, "we can let him go."

...Jean Valjean felt like a man about to faint.

The bishop approached him and said, in a low voice, "Do

not forget, ever, that you have promised me to use this silver to become an honest man."

Jean Valjean, who had no recollection of any such promise, stood dumbfounded. The bishop...continued, solemnly, "...It is your soul I am buying for you." (Victor Hugo, *Les Miserables*)

PRAYER

Grant me the wisdom, Lord,
to respond to the folly around me
with humor and integrity.

CANTICLE Canticle of St. Patrick

Evening Prayer

Begin with page 39.

SCRIPTURE *See page 42.*

REFLECTION

How would you describe the soil in your soul—rich, rocky, hard, soft?

PRAYER

You, God, are the Ground of my being
and the Sower of seed for my soul.

CANTICLE Wisdom Canticle

Morning Prayer

Begin with page 38.

SCRIPTURE Matthew 10:28

And do not be afraid of those who kill the body but
cannot kill the soul; rather, be afraid of the one who can
destroy both body and soul in Gehennna.

COMMENTARY

One of the priests active in the civil rights movement
would constantly remind his audiences to give the poor
more than bread for their body. The poor need bread for
their souls too, he would say.

A good example of this comes from a nun who was
working with a group of women prisoners. She said to
them, "I can teach you how to interview for a job, I can
teach you a skill or I can teach you to dance. Which
would you prefer?" Their overwhelming response was,
"Teach us how to dance." And as they learned to dance,
they discovered their souls.

PRAYER

Lead me, Lord, to that abandon
where I can dance as if I'll never fall
and love as if I'll never hurt.

CANTICLE Canticle of Judith

Evening Prayer

Begin with page 39.

SCRIPTURE *See page 44.*

REFLECTION

What do I do for myself to nourish my soul and my creative potential?

PRAYER

Lord of the Dance,
as my body moves to the rhythm of the universe
I step into that creative chasm
that embraces both Creator and creature.

CANTICLE Canticle of St. Francis

Morning Prayer

Begin with page 38.

SCRIPTURE Matthew 11:23-24

And as for you, Capernaum:

> "Will you be exalted to heaven?
> You will go down to the netherworld."

For if the mighty deeds done in your midst had been done in Sodom, it would have remained until this day. But I tell you, it will be more tolerable for the land of Sodom on the day of judgment than for you.

COMMENTARY

If you are a parent, you can empathize with Christ in today's Scripture. How difficult it is to stand by and see your children make choices that are destructive. Just as parents suffer when their children are in trouble, so Christ is constantly crucified as he witnesses his children taking advantage of, even killing, one another.

PRAYER

Let my fingers, hands and mouth
live up to the faith I proclaim.

Glory be to the Father....

CANTICLE Canticle of Zechariah

Evening Prayer

Begin with page 39.

SCRIPTURE *See page 46.*

REFLECTION

Of the choices I made today, which ones would be
consistent with Christ's choices for me?

PRAYER

Do not get discouraged
or give up on me, God.
Even in my wrong choices,
I remember
that your love is unconditional.

CANTICLE Canticle of Mary

Morning Prayer

Begin with page 38.

SCRIPTURE Matthew 11:30

For my yoke is easy, and my burden light.

PUTTING PRAYER INTO PRACTICE

Today, give Christ your burdens. Let him help you with your cross.

Is your job or ministry so demanding that at times you are not sure you can go on?

Are you ready to give up on a relationship with a loved one?

Have you lost someone who meant so much to you that life has lost its meaning?

Are you in such physical pain that you want to breathe your last breath?

Take all of your anguish and give it to God. He will comfort you. How or in what way is a mystery, but you will receive strength and your burden will be lightened. You may not be comforted in the way you wished or strengthened at the point you anticipated, but you will be able to carry your cross with a sense of peace and fulfillment.

PRAYER

You walk with me, loving Lord,
with your shoulder beneath my cross.
I draw my strength from you.

CANTICLE Canticle of Mary

Evening Prayer

Begin with page 39.

SCRIPTURE *See page 48.*

REFLECTION

What particular situation did I give to God and in what
way was my burden lightened?

PRAYER

You show me,
Brother Jesus,
how to lighten my burden
by letting go of results.
You are gentle and humble of heart.

CANTICLE Wisdom Canticle

Morning Prayer

Begin with page 38.

SCRIPTURE 1 Samuel 16:7b

Do not judge from his appearance or from his lofty
stature, because I have rejected him. Not as man sees
does God see, because man sees the appearance but the
LORD looks into the heart.

PUTTING PRAYER INTO PRACTICE

Look into your heart today and examine your motives.
For instance, an act which appears on the surface to be a
concern for others can often be motivated by a personal
need—to control, to be appreciated, to escape loneliness,
to have power. While no act is one hundred percent pure,
look carefully into your actions today and try to become
aware of which motives are selfish and which are
selfless.

PRAYER

Asleep and unaware,
my soul lies veiled.
Only your touch, God,
awakens my integrity.

CANTICLE Canticle of Mary

Evening Prayer

Begin with page 39.

SCRIPTURE *See page 50.*

REFLECTION

Did I look behind my motions today to discover my real motives? Which motives am I proud of?

PRAYER

You remind me, Yahweh,
to see beyond the surface.
For your wisdom,
which brings new vision,
I sing alleluia!

CANTICLE Canticle of Judith

Morning Prayer

Begin with page 38.

SCRIPTURE Hosea 8:4b-6

> With their silver and gold they made
>   idols for themselves, to their own destruction.
> Cast away your calf, O Samaria!
>   my wrath is kindled against them;
> How long will they be unable to attain
>   innocence in Israel?
> The work of an artisan,
>   no god at all,
> Destined for the flames—
>   such is the calf of Samaria!

COMMENTARY

> The appreciation of fine art is one of the last qualities to
> develop in the evolution of humanity. Too often,
> however, writers, painters, composers and other artists
> fall in love with what they perceive as their own creation,
> losing sight of the fact that they are only a channel for
> God's genius.

PRAYER

> If I do not choose your will,
> Divine Creator,
> I am destined to become
> what I have chosen!

CANTICLE Canticle of Mary

Evening Prayer

Begin with page 39.

SCRIPTURE *See page 52.*

REFLECTION

What are the golden calves in my life?

PRAYER

You do not forsake me
even when I forget you;
your love endures.
My heart is filled with joy
whenever I come back to you.

CANTICLE Canticle of Zechariah

Opening Song for Morning Prayer

SALUTATION

> I awake rejoicing
> happy to live
> in the "land of the free."

SONG Psalm 108:2-6

> My heart is steadfast, O God; my heart is steadfast;
>   I will sing and chant praise.
> Awake, O my soul; awake, lyre and harp.
>   I will wake the dawn.
> I will give thanks to you among the peoples, O LORD;
>   I will chant your praise among the nations,
> For your kindness towers to the heavens,
>   and your faithfulness to the skies.
> Be exalted above the heavens, O God;
>   over all the earth be your glory!

Turn to the page with today's date for the continuation of Morning Prayer.

Opening Song for Evening Prayer

SALUTATION

Your glory, God,
reigns over both the sun and the stars,
the daylight and the dark.

SONG Psalm 108:5-6, 12-14a

Be exalted above the heavens, O God;
  over all the earth be your glory!
That your loved ones may escape,
  help us by your right hand, and answer us.
Have you not, O God, rejected us,
  so that you go not forth, O God, with our armies?
Give us aid against the foe,
  for worthless is the help of men.
Under God we shall do valiantly....

Turn to the page with today's date for the continuation of Evening Prayer.

Morning Prayer

Begin with page 54.

SCRIPTURE Song of Songs 8:6-7

Set me as a seal on your heart,
    as a seal on your arm;
For stern as death is love
    relentless as the nether world is devotion;
    its flames are a blazing fire.
Deep waters cannot quench love,
    nor floods sweep it away.
Were one to offer all he owns to purchase love,
    he would be roundly mocked.

PUTTING PRAYER INTO PRACTICE

Christ loved without judgment. Even though he warned
of the dangers of taking "the selfish path," he invited all
into the embrace of his selfless love. The demands of
unconditional love are great! Be aware, today, of how
judgment interferes with love.

PRAYER

I seek you
and you find me,
Lord of love.
In truth,
we were always one.

CANTICLE Canticle of St. Patrick

Evening Prayer

Begin with page 55.

SCRIPTURE *See page 56.*

REFLECTION

Today, did I allow at least one person the freedom to be without making judgment? What was the result?

Enter your reflections in your spiritual journal, if you are keeping one.

PRAYER

You take my hand and show me
an enchanted forest.
In wonder and glee,
we walk the wooded land.

CANTICLE Canticle of St. Francis

Morning Prayer

Begin with page 54.

SCRIPTURE Matthew 12:48b-50

"Who is my mother? Who are my brothers?" And
stretching out his hand toward his disciples, he said,
"Here are my mother and my brothers. For whoever
does the will of my heavenly Father is my brother, and
sister, and mother."

PUTTING PRAYER INTO PRACTICE

Choice, evidently, is what distinguishes the family of
God from the human family. Watch your choices today.
Do they reflect the will of the Father?

If you are trying to make a decision about something
important, sit in quiet now, and ask what God's will is in
regard to your options.

PRAYER

It is in my choices
that I determine my path.
Only in stillness and quiet
can I discern the way
which leads to you, my God.

CANTICLE Canticle of Mary

Evening Prayer

Begin with page 55.

SCRIPTURE *See page 58.*

REFLECTION

Which of my choices over the last six months have led me closer to God?

PRAYER

Brother Jesus,
you are the beacon
pointing the way
to my Father's house.
You bring light to my days
and joy to my heart!

CANTICLE Canticle of Zechariah

Morning Prayer

Begin with page 54.

SCRIPTURE Micah 7:8-9

Rejoice not over me, O my enemy!
  though I have fallen, I will arise;
  though I sit in darkness, the LORD is my light.
The wrath of the LORD I will endure
  because I have sinned against him,
Until he takes up my cause,
  and establishes my right.
He will bring me forth to the light;
  I will see his justice.

WORDS OF WISDOM

"You are not making a gift to the poor man from your possessions," says St. Ambrose, "but you are returning what is his. For what is common has been given for the use of all, you make exclusive use of it. The earth belongs to all, not to the rich." These words declare that private ownership confers on no one a supreme and unconditional right. No one is allowed to set aside solely for his own advantage possessions which exceed his needs when others lack the necessities of life....

The common good, therefore, at times demands the expropriation of an estate. (Paul VI)[12]

PRAYER

Help me to put away my possessiveness
and to play a part in ordering a just society
that allows each person to meet his or her basic needs.

CANTICLE Canticle of Mary

Evening Prayer

Begin with page 55.

SCRIPTURE *See page 60.*

REFLECTION

Of the many luxuries I have as an American, is there one
I can eliminate so that I can give the savings to someone
in dire need?

PRAYER

Give me a generous heart, O Lord!

CANTICLE Canticle of St. Francis

Morning Prayer

Begin with page 54.

SCRIPTURE Matthew 13:31b-32

The kingdom of heaven is like a mustard seed that a person took and sowed in a field. It is the smallest of all the seeds, yet when full-grown it is the largest of plants. It becomes a large bush, and the birds of the sky come and dwell in its branches.

PUTTING PRAYER INTO PRACTICE

You will be given many opportunities today to use the power of love to overcome difficulties. And the more you develop this gift, the greater the power grows. Respond to at least one of these opportunities and write the details surrounding that response.

Enter your reflections in your spiritual journal, if you are keeping one.

PRAYER

What can I do?
You who planted this seed within,
teach me to tend my garden
so that I may grow and bloom
into the image of your vision.

CANTICLE Wisdom Canticle

Evening Prayer

Begin with page 55.

SCRIPTURE *See page 62.*

REFLECTION

What am I doing, on a daily basis, to nurture that "seed" of the spirit within me?

PRAYER

You give us the seeds
to grow divine forests
and to become ourselves,
flowers of your love.
We sing and rejoice
in our potential.

CANTICLE Canticle of Judith

Morning Prayer

Begin with page 54.

SCRIPTURE Jeremiah 2:12-13

> Be amazed at this, O heavens,
>   and shudder with sheer horror, says the LORD.
> Two evils have my people done:
>   they have forsaken me, the source of living waters;
> They have dug themselves cisterns,
>   broken cisterns, that hold no water.

PUTTING PRAYER INTO PRACTICE

Examine your own use of water today. Find out the facts about this valuable resource and what you can do to become a better steward of this precious life-giving fluid.

According to *Diet for a New America*, half of all water used in America goes to livestock production. Twenty-five gallons of water are needed to produce one pound of wheat whereas 2,500 gallons are needed to produce one pound of meat.[13]

PRAYER

Help me, Giver of all good things,
to live in harmony with the earth,
to take only what I need
and replenish what I take.

CANTICLE Canticle of St. Francis

Evening Prayer

Begin with page 55.

SCRIPTURE *See page 64.*

REFLECTION

Is my diet in harmony with the earth's natural resources?

PRAYER

Bountiful Father,
you give us living waters
and fertile lands.
It is through Mother Earth
that we all are interconnected.
We praise you, Spirit of Creation!

CANTICLE Canticle of Judith

Morning Prayer

Begin with page 54.

SCRIPTURE Matthew 13:24b-26, 30

The kingdom of heaven may be likened to a man who
sowed good seed in his field. While everyone was asleep
his enemy came and sowed weeds all through the wheat,
and then went off. When the crop grew and bore fruit,
the weeds appeared as well.... "Let them grow together
until harvest; then at harvest time I will say to the
harvesters, 'First collect the weeds and tie them into
bundles for burning; but gather the wheat into my
barn.'"

PUTTING PRAYER INTO PRACTICE

Notice the weeds in your own garden. To uproot these
weeds and burn them is a kind of hell—the purging that
St. John of the Cross speaks of in *The Dark Night of the
Soul*.

PRAYER

Send me the stamina and strength,
Gardener of my soul,
to see and uproot the weeds
that are stifling my blooms.

CANTICLE Wisdom Canticle

Evening Prayer

Begin with page 55.

SCRIPTURE *See page 66.*

REFLECTION

What weeds did I discover in my garden?

Enter your reflections in your spiritual journal, if you are keeping one.

PRAYER

Thank you for the sun and soil,
water and wisdom,
to plant and grow gardens of beauty
here on earth.

CANTICLE Canticle of St. Francis

Morning Prayer

Begin with page 54.

SCRIPTURE Luke 10:38-42

As they continued their journey [Jesus] entered a village where a woman whose name was Martha welcomed him. She had a sister named Mary [who] sat beside the Lord at his feet listening to him speak. Martha, burdened with much serving, came to him and said, "Lord, do you not care that my sister has left me by myself to do the serving? Tell her to help me." The Lord said to her in reply, "Martha, Martha, you are anxious and worried about many things. There is need of only one thing. Mary has chosen the better part and it will not be taken from her."

PUTTING PRAYER INTO PRACTICE

If you are living in harmony with God's will, you will certainly lead a full life, but not necessarily a hurried or stressful one. Busyness can be a status symbol for many spiritual seekers. Examine your busyness. Try to separate which action comes out of prayer and which action comes out of compulsion or ego. When your action comes out of prayer, you will feel "in the flow." When your action comes out of compulsion or ego, you will feel like a gerbil on a treadmill. Strive only for that action which comes from prayer.

PRAYER

> Free me, God,
> from the compulsive busyness
> which interferes with
> our prayer relationship.

CANTICLE Canticle of Mary

Evening Prayer

Begin with page 55.

SCRIPTURE *See page 68.*

REFLECTION

What attachments are driving me to frenzied, frantic activity? Can I let go of at least one of these attachments?

PRAYER

> Spirit of grace,
> slow me down.
> Make my steps deliberate,
> my pace unhurried.
> Gratefully,
> I enjoy the present moment.

CANTICLE Wisdom Canticle

Morning Prayer

Begin with page 54.

SCRIPTURE Luke 10:41-42

Martha, Martha, you are anxious and worried about
many things. There is need of only one thing. Mary has
chosen the better part and it will not be taken from her.

PRAYER

Where are you, Soul and Source of life?

Lost in the rush to do good.
Trampled by the triumph of smooth talk!

How did I lose touch with you,
pure and eternal core of my being?

In the ceaseless drum of doing
you grew deaf to my whisper.

And to capture you again,
what price do I pay?

Your life, merely your life.
Lose it in me.

CANTICLE Canticle of St. Patrick

Evening Prayer

Begin with page 55.

SCRIPTURE *See page 70.*

REFLECTION

Do I stop to reflect on what the person I am helping needs, or do I give mainly to meet my own needs?

PRAYER

For a few minutes now, listen to the singing of your own soul—hear the song it is singing to you.

Silence

CANTICLE Wisdom Canticle

Morning Prayer

Begin with page 54.

SCRIPTURE Jeremiah 14:19b-22

Why have you struck us a blow
   that cannot be healed?
We wait for peace, to no avail;
   for a time of healing, but terror comes instead.

We recognize, O LORD, our wickedness,
   the guilt of our fathers;
   that we have sinned against you.
For your name's sake spurn us not,
   disgrace not the throne of your glory;
   remember your covenant with us
      and break it not.

Among the nations' idols is there any that gives rain?
   Or can the mere heavens send showers?
Is it not you alone, O LORD,
   our God, to whom we look?
   You alone have done all these things.

PUTTING PRAYER INTO PRACTICE

If you recognize the error of your actions in some
particular area and ask for God's forgiveness, he will
bring you mercy and healing. But the effects of your
destructive action (smoking, drinking, overeating,
violence, gossip) may be something you have to live with
the rest of your life—may become your cross.

PRAYER

O Lord our God,
even though you forgive my weaknesses,
I am aware that I must still struggle
with the consequences of my actions.
In every decision I make today,
may I choose your way.

CANTICLE Canticle of Mary

Evening Prayer

Begin with page 55.

SCRIPTURE *See page 72.*

REFLECTION

What difficulties or afflictions are in my life as a result of
poor decisions and actions?

PRAYER

You give us the grace,
Holy Spirit,
to make choices that will have
positive, life-giving consequences.
We praise your wisdom.

CANTICLE Wisdom Canticle

Morning Prayer

Begin with page 54.

SCRIPTURE 1 Corinthians 10:31-33

So whether you eat or drink, or whatever you do, do
everything for the glory of God. Avoid giving offense,
whether to Jews or Greeks or the church of God, just as
I try to please everyone in every way, not seeking my
own benefit but that of the many, that they may be saved.

COMMENTARY

Observe today how the Lord diverts you from your
normal path. What do these diversions mean and what
may God be saying to you through them?

PRAYER

Accept, O Lord, all my freedom.
Accept my memory, my mind and all my will.
Give me only your love and your grace
and I am rich enough,
and I ask nothing more. (Ignatius of Loyola)

CANTICLE Canticle of Zechariah

Evening Prayer

Begin with page 55.

SCRIPTURE *See page 74.*

REFLECTION

How much liberty do I give God in my life?

PRAYER

My one true need is your love,
which you give so abundantly.

Glory be to the Father....

CANTICLE Canticle of Mary

Notes

[1] The excerpt from the 1989 *Song of the Earth Calendar*, copyright ©1989 by Sister Mary Southard, is reprinted with the permission of the author.

[2] This excerpt from *Rerum Novarum* (1891), #31-32, 76, was taken from *Justice in the Marketplace*, National Conference of Catholic Bishops/United States Catholic Conference, copyright ©1985, and is used with the permission of the publisher.

[3] This excerpt from *Quadregesimo Anno* (1931), #46, 109, was taken from *Justice in the Marketplace*, National Conference of Catholic Bishops/United States Catholic Conference, copyright ©1985, and is used with permission of the publisher.

[4] This excerpt from *The Prayer of the Frog: A Book of Story Meditations*, 1st Volume, copyright ©1988 by Anthony de Mello, S.J., is reprinted with permission of Gujarat Sahitya Prakash, Anand, India.

[5] The excerpt from *Breakthrough: Meister Eckhart's Creation Spirituality* by Matthew Fox, O.P., copyright ©1980 by Image Books, is reprinted with permission of the publisher, Doubleday.

[6] Facts excerpted from *Diet for a New America*, by John Robbins, copyright ©1987, are reprinted with the permission of the author.

[7] The excerpt from the 1989 *Song of the Earth Calendar*, copyright ©1989 by Sister Mary Southard, is reprinted with the permission of the author.

[8] The excerpt from the 1989 *Song of the Earth Calendar*, copyright ©1989 by Sister Mary Southard, is reprinted with the permission of the author.

[9] The excerpt from the 1989 *Song of the Earth Calendar*, copyright ©1989 by Sister Mary Southard, is reprinted with the permission of the author.

[10] This excerpt from *Mater et Magistra* (1961), #157-158, was taken from *Justice in the Marketplace*, National Conference of Catholic Bishops/United States Catholic Conference, copyright ©1985, and is used with permission of the publisher.

[11] The excerpt from *Addiction and Grace*, by Gerald C. May, M.D., copyright ©1988 by Gerald C. May, is reprinted by permission of the publisher, HarperSanFrancisco.

[12] This excerpt from *Populorum Progressio* (1967), #23-24, was taken from *Justice in the Marketplace*, National Conference of Catholic Bishops/United States Catholic Conference, copyright ©1985 and is used with permission.

[13] Facts excerpted from *Diet for a New America*, by John Robbins, copyright ©1987, are reprinted with the permission of the author.

August

Opening Song for Morning Prayer

SALUTATION

God of Morning,
capture me in your embrace
as I step over the threshold
of a new day.

SONG Psalm 8:2-5

O LORD, our Lord,
how glorious is your name over all the earth!
You have exalted your majesty above the heavens.
Out of the mouths of babes and sucklings
you have fashioned praise because of your foes,
to silence the hostile and the vengeful.
When I behold your heavens, the work of your fingers,
the moon and stars which you have set in place—
What is man that you should be mindful of him,
or the son of man that you should care for him?

Turn to the page with today's date for the continuation of Morning Prayer.

Opening Song for Evening Prayer

SALUTATION

God of Twilight,
be with me now
at the hour of dusk,
as I seek your refreshing caress!

SONG Psalm 8:6-10

You have made him little less than the angels
  and crowned him with glory and honor.
You have given him rule over the works of your hands,
  putting all things under his feet:

All sheep and oxen,
  yes, and the beasts of the field,
The birds of the air, the fishes of the sea,
  and whatever swims the paths of the seas.

O LORD, our Lord,
  how glorious is your name over all the earth!

Turn to the page with today's date for the continuation of Evening Prayer.

Morning Prayer

Begin with page 78.

SCRIPTURE Jeremiah 18:3-6

I went down to the potter's house and there he was,
working at the wheel. Whenever the object of clay which
he was making turned out badly in his hands, he tried
again, making of the clay another object of whatever sort
he pleased. Then the word of the Lord came to me: Can
I not do to you, house of Israel, as this potter has done?
says the LORD. Indeed, like clay in the hand of the potter,
so are you in my hand, house of Israel.

PUTTING PRAYER INTO PRACTICE

Pick a few ways that you can be a vessel for God's
compassion.

PRAYER

Mold me into your masterpiece,
original Artist and Designer of the universe,
for it is only in your hands
that I will reach my divine destiny!

CANTICLE Canticle of St. Patrick

Evening Prayer

Begin with page 79.

SCRIPTURE *See page 80.*

REFLECTION

How did I show kindness and concern for others today?

PRAYER

You imbue me
with life, breath, beauty and form.
I clap my hands and shout for joy
in honor and praise of your name,
creator God.

CANTICLE Canticle of Judith

Morning Prayer

Begin with page 78.

SCRIPTURE Matthew 13:44

> The kingdom of heaven is like a treasure buried in a field, which a person finds and hides again, and out of joy goes and sells all that he has and buys that field.

MEDITATION EXERCISE

Christ is not telling us how to get into heaven but how to get heaven into us. If we only knew what Christ knew, we would be willing to give up everything else to protect it.

One of the best ways to find this "treasure within" is through prayer and silence. When we have inner peace, it is easier to recognize, understand and connect with the God within. Take this thought into silent meditation. If it would help, you could try repeating the words "God within" in rhythm with your breathing. As you say "God," inhale. As you say "within," exhale. As you breathe out, imagine you are expelling fear and selfishness. Practice this now for a few minutes. End the silence with the Lord's Prayer.

CANTICLE Wisdom Canticle

Evening Prayer

Begin with page 79.

SCRIPTURE *See page 82.*

REFLECTION

Can I go to a place within me and find a touch of heaven?

PRAYER

You who dwell within,
you who are the source,
you are my treasure!

CANTICLE Canticle of Mary

Morning Prayer

Begin with page 78.

SCRIPTURE Matthew 13:47-50

Again, the kingdom of heaven is like a net thrown into
the sea, which collects fish of every kind. When it is full
they haul it ashore and sit down to put what is good into
buckets. What is bad they throw away. Thus it will be at
the end of the age. The angels will go out and separate
the wicked from the righteous and throw them into the
fiery furnace, where there will be wailing and grinding of
teeth.

REFLECTION

What mix of good and bad is in the net of myself? What
do I need to throw away? What can I offer as
nourishment to another?

PRAYER

People cannot live by bread alone
but neither can they live on prayer.
Guide me, Giver of all good things,
to seek your treasure
in a balanced, wholesome way.

CANTICLE Canticle of St. Francis

Evening Prayer

Begin with page 79.

SCRIPTURE *See page 84.*

REFLECTION

What role does sacrifice play in my life? For whom or what do I sacrifice?

PRAYER

Brother Jesus,
you remind us of our roots.
From a compassionate, caring Creator
we were brought forth
and given the key to eternity.

CANTICLE Canticle of Zechariah

Morning Prayer

Begin with page 78.

SCRIPTURE Ephesians 6:18a

With all prayer and supplication, pray at every
opportunity in the Spirit.

WORDS OF WISDOM

Let us always desire the happy life from the Lord God
and always pray for it. But for this very reason we turn
our mind to the task of prayer at appointed hours, since
that desire grows lukewarm, so to speak, from our
involvement in other concerns and occupations. We
remind ourselves through the words of prayer to focus
our attention on the object of our desire; otherwise, the
desire that began to grow lukewarm may grow chill
altogether and may be totally extinguished unless it is
repeatedly stirred into flame. (St. Augustine) [1]

PRAYER

It is not simple, Spirit divine,
to put away the occupations of the world
and fall, absorbed, into prayer.
Lukewarm though I am,
inflame me with your fire.

CANTICLE Canticle of Mary

Evening Prayer

Begin with page 79.

SCRIPTURE *See page 86.*

REFLECTION

Am I satisfied with my prayer routine? Is it providing me with enough spiritual nourishment?

PRAYER

Thank you for your spark
of fire and light,
God of creation!

CANTICLE Canticle of St. Francis

Morning Prayer

Begin with page 78.

SCRIPTURE John 6:8-10a, 11

One of his disciples, Andrew, the brother of Simon Peter, said to him, "There is a boy here who has five barley loaves and two fish; but what good are these for so many?" Jesus said, "Have the people recline." ...So the men reclined, about five thousand in number. Then Jesus took the loaves, gave thanks, and distributed them to those who were reclining, and also as much of the fish as they wanted.

PUTTING PRAYER INTO PRACTICE

Because the boy in the crowd gave Jesus five loaves and two fish, Jesus was able to use this gift and multiply it to feed thousands. Each day, we are asked to give something so that Christ can multiply it and use it to nurture others. Watch for those times today and respond.

PRAYER

It is a mystery to me, Lord,
why you need my time, money or skill
to build your kingdom,
but only when I give
from my humble cupboard
are you able to turn my gift
into a banquet.

CANTICLE Canticle of St. Patrick

Evening Prayer

Begin with page 79.

SCRIPTURE *See page 88.*

REFLECTION

> Do I give only when all my needs (or my family's needs) are satisfied?

PRAYER

> The more I give away in your name, Lord,
> the more I enable you to fill my emptiness.
> Glory be to your name!

CANTICLE Canticle of Judith

Morning Prayer

Begin with page 78.

SCRIPTURE Matthew 6:26a

Look at the birds of the air, they do not sow or reap, they gather nothing into barns, yet your heavenly Father feeds them.

PUTTING PRAYER INTO PRACTICE

An attitude of leisure or prayer brings harmony to situations which could otherwise be tense. You can experience the truth of this next time you are engaged in controversy. Try entering the conversation with a sense of play. Follow these simple rules: Withhold judgment. Whatever your opinion, don't jump into the discussion to defend it. Start by listening to the other's point of view. Ask questions. Choose your words carefully: Use only those that convey respect. Learn as much as you can. When it is time to express your opinion (wait until asked), casually and playfully say, "Well, I see it this way. What do you think?"

You'll be amazed at how much fun conflict can be if you keep the mood playful and remain detached.

PRAYER

I squander myself
in the pleasures of your creation
and serendipitously stumble upon you,
my Maker.

CANTICLE Canticle of Judith

Evening Prayer

Begin with page 79.

SCRIPTURE *See page 90.*

REFLECTION

Think of the times you have been in touch with the wonder and awe of the universe.

PRAYER

For the grace to abandon my fears
and lose myself in the unknown,
I thank you, Creator God.

CANTICLE Canticle of St. Francis

Morning Prayer

Begin with page 78.

SCRIPTURE John 1:9, 12-13

The true light, which enlightens everyone, was coming
into the world.... [T]o those who did accept him he gave
power to become children of God, to those who believe
in his name, who were born not by natural generation
nor by human choice nor by a man's decision but of God.

WORDS OF WISDOM

I am all at once what Christ is, since he
   was what I am, and
This Jack, joke, poor potsherd, patch,
   matchwood, immortal diamond,
   Is immortal diamond.[2]

PRAYER

In my natural state,
I am a princess or prince,
inheriting the created world
from you, my Father, who art in heaven.
Help me see through my own distortions of reality,
caused by bad experiences and negative thoughts,
which create barriers to the storehouse of wisdom,
my natural birthright.

CANTICLE Wisdom Canticle

Evening Prayer

Begin with page 79.

SCRIPTURE *See page 92.*

REFLECTION

Do I believe I am "inherently" good? Am I able to set
aside negative experiences and thoughts (bad moods) so
that I can cope in a positive manner?

PRAYER

You created in me
a positive core of integrity
and daily you give me
the grace to tap into this core
through quiet prayer and discipline.
You, God, are the divine essence of all things!

CANTICLE Canticle of Mary

Opening Song for Morning Prayer

SALUTATION

Awake and arise my beloved child!
I give you this day as a precious gift.
Unwrap its mystery and delight in its treasure.

SONG Psalm 148:1-5

Praise the LORD from the heavens,
   praise him in the heights;
Praise him, all you his angels,
   praise God, all you his hosts.
Praise him, sun and moon;
   praise all you shining stars.
Praise him, you highest heavens,
   and you waters above the heavens.
Let them praise the name of the LORD,
   for he commanded and they were created....

Turn to the page with today's date for the continuation of Morning Prayer.

Opening Song for Evening Prayer

SALUTATION

The night holds a promise
to those who wait in stillness
and welcome the unknown.

SONG Psalm 148:7-13a

Praise the LORD from the earth,
  you sea monsters and all depths,
Fire and hail, snow and mist,
  storm winds that fulfill his word;
You mountains and all you hills,
  you fruit trees and all you cedars;
You wild beasts and all tame animals,
  you creeping things and you winged fowl.

Let the kings of the earth and all peoples,
  the princes and all the judges of the earth,
Young men too, and maidens,
  old men and boys,
Praise the name of the LORD....

Turn to the page with today's date for the continuation of Evening Prayer.

Morning Prayer

Begin with page 94.

SCRIPTURE Matthew 16:26

What profit would there be for one to gain the whole world and forfeit his life? Or what can one give in exchange for his life?

WORDS OF WISDOM

Have charity for one another. Guard humility. Make your treasure out of voluntary poverty. (St. Dominic, from his deathbed)

PRAYER

It is only through humility and simplicity that I can find the sacred in my life.

CANTICLE Canticle of Mary

Evening Prayer

Begin with page 95.

SCRIPTURE *See page 96.*

REFLECTION

In what ways did I move in harmony with the divine will?
In what ways did I disrupt God's plan for me because I
wanted to do things my way?

PRAYER

For St. Dominic
and his shining spirit,
we are grateful,
Lord, God, Giver of all good things.

CANTICLE Canticle of St. Francis

Morning Prayer

Begin with page 94.

SCRIPTURE Matthew 16:15-20

He said to them, "But who do you say that I am?" Simon
Peter said in reply, "You are the Messiah, the Son of the
living God." Jesus said to him in reply, "Blessed are you,
Simon son of Jonah. For flesh and blood has not revealed
this to you, but my heavenly Father. And so I say to you,
you are Peter, and upon this rock I will build my church,
and the gates of the netherworld shall not prevail against
it. I will give you the keys to the kingdom of heaven.
Whatever you bind on earth shall be bound in heaven;
and whatever you loose on earth shall be loosed in
heaven."

COMMENTARY

Possibly, the keys to the kingdom symbolize love (God's
love, not human love). Whoever builds on that love has
already, in a sense, entered the kingdom of God; and
whatever is built on the foundation of love will be
imperishable.

PRAYER

Church of majesty,
Church of human error,
in both your light and dark hours
you have the words of eternal life!

CANTICLE Wisdom Canticle

Evening Prayer

Begin with page 95.

SCRIPTURE *See page 98.*

REFLECTION

What things in my life am I doing out of love?

PRAYER

You show me the kingdom,
Brother Jesus,
and give me the key.
But I get sidetracked
by my own personal empire.
In spite of my distractions,
you are my final desire, Lord.

CANTICLE Canticle of Zechariah

Morning Prayer

Begin with page 94.

SCRIPTURE Luke 14:27-30

Whoever does not carry his own cross and come after me
cannot be my disciple. Which of you wishing to construct
a tower does not first sit down and calculate the cost to
see if there is enough for its completion? Otherwise,
after laying the foundation and finding himself unable to
finish the work the onlookers should laugh at him and
say, "This one began to build but did not have the
resources to finish."

PUTTING PRAYER INTO PRACTICE

When a man goes to build a house, he takes an inventory
of the materials he has on hand and decides if they are
good or right for the building. What is inferior he casts
aside and does without or replaces from another source.
And you should, in building your character, cast aside
the inferior qualities. Do not dwell on any inadequacy;
just gently set it aside and build on the good materials
you find in yourself. Do not let your faults disturb you.
When you find yourself dwelling on mistakes or
weaknesses, distract yourself and look again upon your
goodness and strength.

PRAYER

Growing upward and pushing onward
I approach you, my Creator,
and gain the grace
to grow beyond my limitations.

CANTICLE Canticle of St. Patrick

Evening Prayer

Begin with page 95.

SCRIPTURE *See page 100.*

REFLECTION What are my good qualities?

Enter your reflections in your spiritual journal, if you are keeping one.

PRAYER Revelation 3:8

I know your works (behold I have left an open door before you, which no one can close). You have limited strength, and yet you have kept my words and have not denied my name.

CANTICLE Canticle of Mary

Morning Prayer

Begin with page 94.

SCRIPTURE Matthew 17:21b

Amen, I say to you, if you have faith the size of a mustard
seed, you will say to this mountain, "Move from here to
there," and it will move. Nothing will be impossible for
you.

PUTTING PRAYER INTO PRACTICE

St. Clare was inspired by St. Francis of Assisi. She lived
her whole life in prayer, putting into practice the gospel
ideals of holy poverty. According to legend, near the end
of her life the entire countryside around the convent
where Clare and her nuns lived was being ravaged and
terrorized by invading soldiers. When they came to the
cloister and pounded on the door, Clare sent her sisters
to their cells and quietly greeted the soldiers at the door
with the Blessed Sacrament in her hand. Stunned by the
simplicity and faith of this fragile woman, the soldiers
departed, leaving the nuns and the convent in peace.

PRAYER

Is it possible for one person,
united with the divine in prayer,
to act as a conduit
for the forces of all creation?

CANTICLE Canticle of St. Patrick

Evening Prayer

Begin with page 95.

SCRIPTURE *See page 102.*

REFLECTION

In which areas of my life have I let go of my will and
turned the results over to God?

PRAYER

You give me the power
to create a landscape of love,
building mountains of mercy
over pits of despair.
Joyfully, I praise your name!

CANTICLE Canticle of St. Francis

Morning Prayer

Begin with page 94.

SCRIPTURE Mark 10:14b-15

Let the children come to me; do not prevent them, for
the kingdom of God belongs to such as these. Amen, I
say to you, whoever does not accept the kingdom of God
like a child will not enter it.

PUTTING PRAYER INTO PRACTICE

It is difficult for us to play with our concepts of God. But
it is that playful spirituality that brings God's gentle
presence into our dialogue with each other. Isn't it true
that God approaches us in the form of a whisper rather
than a loud shout? And that may be the cue for how we
should approach one another.

PRAYER

As a humble child
seeking to unravel the mysteries of the universe,
I can discover you, God,
only as I let go of my personal notions
and toy with the possibilities expressed by others.

CANTICLE Canticle of Judith

Evening Prayer

Begin with page 95.

SCRIPTURE *See page 104.*

REFLECTION

In what ways can I cultivate a childlike sense of wonder?

PRAYER

God, you are in the face
of everyone I met today,
but I'm often too proud or too adult
to see the kingdom
that surrounds me.

CANTICLE Canticle of St. Francis

Morning Prayer

Begin with page 94.

SCRIPTURE Matthew 18:3b-4, 10-12

Amen, I say to you, unless you turn and become like children, you will not enter the kingdom of heaven. Whoever humbles himself like this child is the greatest in the kingdom of heaven....

See that you do not despise one of these little ones, for I say to you that their angels in heaven always look upon the face of my heavenly Father. What is your opinion? If a man has a hundred sheep and one of them goes astray, will he not leave the ninety-nine in the hills and go in search of the stray?

PUTTING PRAYER INTO PRACTICE

A child lives more out of the heart than the head. As we grow up, we tend to rely more on logic than on love. The man who leaves ninety-nine sheep to find the stray is motivated by love. Someone motivated by logic would probably protect the ninety-nine at hand rather than risk the safety of the whole flock to find a stray.

Think of some way you can become like a child today. Be clear about this while you are in prayer so that when the occasion arises, you will be able to put your good intentions into practice.

PRAYER

You call us to become children again,

rather than remain in our childhood.

For it is only the soul that is taught by experience,
graced with wisdom and humbled by divine love
that can return to innocence.

CANTICLE Canticle of Mary

Evening Prayer

Begin with page 95.

SCRIPTURE *See page 106.*

REFLECTION

How can I incorporate more childlike simplicity and
humility into my life?

PRAYER

Stay close, O soul, to the shepherd's song,
for his melody makes the heart sing.

CANTICLE Canticle of Judith

Morning Prayer

Begin with page 94.

SCRIPTURE Matthew 22:36-40

"Teacher, which commandment in the law is the greatest?" [Jesus] said to him, "You shall love the Lord, your God, with all your heart, with all your soul, and with all your mind. This is the greatest and the first commandment. The second is like it: You shall love your neighbor as yourself. The whole law and the prophets depend on these two commandments."

PUTTING PRAYER INTO PRACTICE

Maximilian Kolbe is an outstanding example of loving your neighbor as yourself. In a Nazi prison camp, he volunteered his life to spare the life of another. During a routine execution round-up, one of the men selected to die pleaded for his life because he had a family to support. Father Kolbe asked to take his place and was subsequently put to death.

PRAYER

You breathed life into me,
divine Creator.
Now I place my heart, soul and mind
at your disposal
to use as you will.

CANTICLE Canticle of St. Patrick

Evening Prayer

Begin with page 95.

SCRIPTURE *See page 108.*

REFLECTION

Was there one way today that I loved my neighbor as
myself?

PRAYER

I celebrate all those
who give their lives for love.
I end my prayer
In gratitude to you,
Brother Jesus.

CANTICLE Canticle of Zechariah

Opening Song for Morning Prayer

SALUTATION

> Let the whole world awake
> to the voice of the Creator
> and joyfully sing
> the hymn of the universe.

SONG Psalm 149:1-5a

> Sing to the LORD a new song
>   of praise in the assembly of the faithful.
> Let Israel be glad in their maker,
>   let the children of Zion rejoice in their king.
> Let them praise his name in the festive dance,
>   let them sing praise to him with timbrel and harp.
> For the LORD loves his people,
>   and he adorns the lowly with victory.
> Let the faithful exult in glory....

Turn to the page with today's date for the continuation of Morning Prayer.

Opening Song for Evening Prayer

SALUTATION

Blessed is the night
that finds me at peace
with the decisions of the day.

SONG Psalm 134:1-3

Come, bless the LORD,
   all you servants of the LORD
Who stand in the house of the LORD
   during the hours of night.
Lift up your hands toward the sanctuary,
   and bless the LORD.
May the LORD bless you from Zion,
   the maker of heaven and earth.

Turn to the page with today's date for the continuation of Evening Prayer.

Morning Prayer

Begin with page 110.

SCRIPTURE Luke 1:39-45

During those days Mary set out and traveled to the hill country in haste to a town of Judah, where she entered the house of Zechariah and greeted Elizabeth. When Elizabeth heard Mary's greeting, the infant leaped in her womb, and Elizabeth, filled with the Holy Spirit, cried out in a loud voice and said, "Most blessed are you among women, and blessed is the fruit of your womb. And how does this happen to me, that the mother of my Lord should come to me? For at the moment the sound of your greeting reached my ears, the infant in my womb leaped for joy. Blessed are you who believed that what was spoken to you by the Lord would be fulfilled."

COMMENTARY

St. Thomas Aquinas and St. Bonaventure argued over whether Mary died a natural death. Was Mary, whose body had been spared the stigma of original sin, also spared from physical death? Was she, while in a bodily sleep, assumed into heaven to live and reign with her son, Christ? The argument has never been definitively settled. Beyond the theological significance, Dr. Carl Jung, noted for his work with the spiritualized collective unconscious, suggests that the symbolism of Mary's being spared death elevates and venerates the "female" aspect of the Godhead.

PRAYER

I am at peace with the emptiness,
the nothingness of my nature,
for it is within that void
that the seed of love
is conceived and brought to birth.

CANTICLE Canticle of Mary

Evening Prayer

Begin with page 111.

SCRIPTURE *See page 112.*

REFLECTION

In what way is the Lord waiting for me to say yes?

PRAYER

Like Mary,
may I grow in gratefulness
for the great things you have given me,
glorious God!

CANTICLE Canticle of Mary

Morning Prayer

Begin with page 110.

SCRIPTURE Luke 12:35-40

Gird your loins and light your lamps and be like servants
who await their master's return from a wedding, ready to
open immediately when he comes and knocks. Blessed
are those servants whom the master finds vigilant on his
arrival. Amen, I say to you, he will gird himself, have
them recline at table, and proceed to wait on them. And
should he come in the second or third watch and find
them prepared in this way, blessed are those servants.
Be sure of this: if the master of the house had known the
hour when the thief was coming, he would not have let
his house be broken into. You also must be prepared, for
at an hour you do not expect, the Son of Man will come.

PUTTING PRAYER INTO PRACTICE

We are asleep to the Spirit, numbed by worldly illusion
and the desire for material comfort. The media, too, drug us
with visual images and advertising gimmicks. Be aware of
the times today when you give in to laziness by
skimming the surface and refusing to delve into the
cause and effect of things.

PRAYER

May I see this day
as a blessed collection of hours,
each one unfolding as it flows
in rhythm with its divine destiny.

CANTICLE Canticle of Judith

Evening Prayer

Begin with page 111.

SCRIPTURE Luke 12:40a

You also must be prepared....

REFLECTION

Do I keep my lamps burning? Am I afire with compassion for my fellow human beings?

PRAYER

For the grace, God,
to be awake and aware,
I am grateful.

CANTICLE Canticle of Mary

Morning Prayer

Begin with page 110.

SCRIPTURE Matthew 19:9

I say to you, whoever divorces his wife (unless the
marriage is unlawful) and marries another commits
adultery.

COMMENTARY

Leo Tolstoy maintained that this passage has been
repeatedly mistranslated. The original meaning,
according to Tolstoy, was not to allow divorce because
the person being divorced (the rejected party) would
turn to adultery.

PRAYER

Lamb of God,
help me to realize the devastation I sow
when I openly reject or fail to affirm another.

CANTICLE Canticle of St. Patrick

Evening Prayer

Begin with page 111.

SCRIPTURE *See page 116.*

REFLECTION

Which people in my life are suffering from my rejection or resentment? What steps can I take to be more accepting of others?

PRAYER

You are faithful and respectful to me, heavenly Father.
Without you, I am overwhelmed with weakness.
Do not divorce yourself from me.

CANTICLE Canticle of Zechariah

Morning Prayer

Begin with page 110.

SCRIPTURE Joshua 24:15

> If it does not please you to serve the LORD, decide today
> whom you will serve, the gods your fathers served
> beyond the River or the gods of the Amorites in whose
> country you are dwelling. As for me and my household,
> we will serve the LORD.

PUTTING PRAYER INTO PRACTICE

> As you make choices today, think each time about whom
> you want to serve. Whenever you are faced with a
> decision, ask yourself which course of action would
> serve God and which would serve self.

PRAYER

> How easy it is,
> gentle God,
> to push you into the corner,
> paying homage only at crucial times
> such as crisis, illness or death.

CANTICLE Canticle of St. Patrick

Evening Prayer

Begin with page 111.

SCRIPTURE *See page 118.*

REFLECTION

Which of my decisions today served God?

PRAYER

Long before I recognized
my own power of choice,
you chose me, Lord.

CANTICLE Canticle of Mary

Morning Prayer

Begin with page 110.

SCRIPTURE Mark 8:22-25

When they arrived at Bethsaida, they brought to him a blind man and begged him to touch him. He took the blind man by the hand and led him outside the village. Putting spittle on his eyes he laid his hands on him and asked, "Do you see anything?" Looking up he replied, "I see people looking like trees and walking." Then he laid hands on his eyes a second time and he saw clearly; his sight was restored and he could see everything distinctly.

WORDS OF WISDOM

Every time I entered into heightened awareness I could not cease marveling at the difference between my two sides. I always felt as if a veil had been lifted from my eyes, as if I had been partially blind before and now I could see. The freedom, the sheer joy that used to possess me on these occasions cannot be compared with anything else I have ever experienced. Yet, at the same time, there was a frightening feeling of sadness and longing that went hand in hand with that freedom and joy. It seems that there is no completeness without sadness and longing, for without them there is no sobriety, no kindness. Wisdom without kindness and knowledge without sobriety are useless. (Carlos Castañeda)[3]

PRAYER

My eyes are blurred with preconceived sight.
Prejudice, programming and my limited perception
hinder my ability to see things as they are.
Give me the vision, God,
to look upon creation with wisdom and kindness,
knowledge and sobriety.

CANTICLE Wisdom Canticle

Evening Prayer

Begin with page 111.

SCRIPTURE *See page 120.*

REFLECTION

How do I look upon the world?

PRAYER

Brother Jesus,
with your healing hand you anoint my eyes
and remove the veil from my vision.

CANTICLE Canticle of Zechariah

Morning Prayer

Begin with page 110.

SCRIPTURE Matthew 19:21

Jesus said to him, "If you wish to be perfect, go, sell what you have and give to [the] poor, and you will have treasure in heaven. Then come, follow me."

COMMENTARY

Christ calls everyone to keep the commandments, but only those who would "be perfect" are encouraged to sell their possessions, give to the poor and follow Christ.

PRAYER

You do not expect perfection,
but you show me the road
to total transformation—
if I choose to journey that far.

CANTICLE Wisdom Canticle

Evening Prayer

Begin with page 111.

SCRIPTURE *See page 122.*

REFLECTION

Do I strive for perfection or am I content to keep the
commandments?

PRAYER

Blessed are you, Creator God,
for you do not lay heavy burdens on me.
You give me choices and opportunities.
You are generous and glorious;
I praise your name!
I stand in awe of your loving presence.
Alleluia!

CANTICLE Canticle of St. Francis

Morning Prayer

Begin with page 110.

SCRIPTURE Matthew 19:23-24, 29-30

Then Jesus said to his disciples, "Amen I say to you, it will be hard for one who is rich to enter the kingdom of heaven. Again I say to you, it is easier for a camel to pass through the eye of a needle than for one who is rich to enter the kingdom of God.... And everyone who has given up houses or brothers or sisters or father or mother or children or lands for the sake of my name will receive a hundred times more, and will inherit eternal life."

COMMENTARY

Why is this theme repeated so often in the Bible? Is it so hard to be rich and good at the same time? Is it possible that Christ is talking about accumulation or an oversupply of anything? Whatever one possesses in abundance—knowledge, wealth, time, creative genius— one is obliged to share. The person who shares continually is not rich in anything because such a person keeps passing on the wealth to others.

PRAYER

Lord Jesus,
I do not know the hour appointed
for me to come to paradise;
but while I am here,
let me live and share

my earthly treasure
as if there were no tomorrow.

CANTICLE Canticle of St. Patrick

Evening Prayer

Begin with page 111.

SCRIPTURE *See page 124.*

REFLECTION

In what ways am I rich? In what ways do I pass along my wealth and in what ways do I hoard it?

PRAYER

Brother Jesus,
you nourish and sustain me
with the words of eternal life,
but my palate often prefers
the sweets of temporal delights.

CANTICLE Wisdom Canticle

Opening Song for Morning Prayer

SALUTATION

With a song,
my soul awakens
to greet the new day.

SONG Psalm 98:1-3

Sing to the LORD a new song,
  for he has done wondrous deeds;
His right hand has won victory for him,
  his holy arm.
The LORD has made his salvation known,
  in the sight of the nations he has revealed his justice.
He has remembered his kindness and his faithfulness
  toward the house of Israel.
All the ends of the earth have seen
  the salvation by our God.

Turn to the page with today's date for the continuation of Morning Prayer.

Opening Song for Evening Prayer

SALUTATION

You who paint the sunsets
and compose celestial refrains,
bring salvation as well as beauty
to the children of the earth!

SONG Psalm 98:4-9

Sing joyfully to the LORD, all you lands,
    break into song; sing praise.
Sing praise to the LORD with the harp,
    with the harp and melodious song.
With trumpets and the sound of the horn,
    sing joyfully before the King, the LORD.

Let the sea and what fills it resound,
    the world and those who dwell in it;
Let the rivers clap their hands,
    the mountains shout with them for joy
Before the LORD, for he comes,
    for he comes to rule the earth;
He will rule the world with justice
    and the peoples with equity.

Turn to the page with today's date for the continuation of Evening Prayer.

Morning Prayer

Begin with page 126.

SCRIPTURE Matthew 20:16

The last will be first and the first will be last.

PUTTING PRAYER INTO PRACTICE

So often the values of the Kingdom of God are portrayed as a flip-flop of earthly values. Watch for ways today that you can reverse worldly ways of "seeing."

PRAYER

Beyond appearances, carry me,
divine Spirit.
You who preside over the universe,
help me strive for a cosmic approach.
Broaden my outlook to include the invisible
so that I might see
the first in the last
and the last in the first.

CANTICLE Wisdom Canticle

Evening Prayer

Begin with page 127.

SCRIPTURE Matthew 20:16

The last will be first and the first will be last.

REFLECTION

In my day-to-day existence, what do I put last that should be first?

PRAYER

Only you, Infinite One,
can set priorities and guide my feet
as they journey toward you.
Give me the vision to stay on course,
so that I may arrive safely
at the many mansions within your house.

CANTICLE Canticle of Zechariah

Morning Prayer

Begin with page 126.

SCRIPTURE Matthew 22:19b-22

Then they handed him the Roman coin. [Jesus] said to
them, "Whose image is this and whose inscription?"
They replied, "Caesar's." At that he said to them, "Then
repay to Caesar what belongs to Caesar and to God what
belongs to God." When they heard this they were
amazed, and leaving him they went away.

PUTTING PRAYER INTO PRACTICE

August is a time for vacations. People vacationing at the
seashore or in the mountains wish for a room with a
view. A view is not only refreshing and enjoyable; it also
provides vision and perspective on one's surroundings.
Scripture acts in the same way: It gives us perspective or
a view of life. Think about how this Gospel passage helps
shape your view of life and gives direction to your
choices.

PRAYER

Through this Scripture passage,
God and Creator,
lead me to a deeper knowledge of you
and my responsibilities here on earth
as a citizen in the City of God.

CANTICLE Canticle of St. Patrick

Evening Prayer

Begin with page 127.

SCRIPTURE *See page 130.*

REFLECTION

How did I integrate today's Scripture into my life?

PRAYER

Lord of light,
you give value to every human life.
Thank you
for lifting me from the darkness of indifference.

CANTICLE Canticle of Zechariah

Morning Prayer

Begin with page 126.

SCRIPTURE Sirach 6:18-21

My son, from your youth embrace discipline,
thus you will find wisdom with graying hair.
As though plowing and sowing, draw close to her;
then await her bountiful crops.
For in cultivating her you will labor but little,
and soon you will eat of her fruits.
How irksome she is to the unruly!
The fool cannot abide her.

PUTTING PRAYER INTO PRACTICE

The discipline of prayer creates the groundwork for a positive attitude and good feelings. Thoughts create moods. A bad mood gets us locked into our personal point of view and allows the ego to rear up with its "I'd rather be right than happy" approach. Today, when you are feeling negative or thinking you are the only one who is right, relax. Slow down. Don't be so serious and don't push ahead. Discipline yourself to let go of negative thoughts. Read a psalm or a poem, listen to some beautiful music, go for a walk, pray, do anything to regain your positive attitude.

PRAYER

It is when I am happy and positive, Lord,
that I am a channel of your love.
Protect me from my own negative thoughts and feelings,
which block the flow of your divine grace.

CANTICLE Canticle of Mary

Evening Prayer

Begin with page 127.

SCRIPTURE *See page 132.*

REFLECTION

How do my daily actions fit into God's grand scheme for
me? How does my negativity interfere with these
actions?

PRAYER

Nothing is more delicious
than the fruit of that tree
which is planted with love
and tended with discipline.

CANTICLE Wisdom Canticle

Morning Prayer

Begin with page 126.

SCRIPTURE Ezekiel 37:4b-6

Dry bones, hear the word of the LORD! Thus says the Lord GOD to these bones: See! I will bring spirit into you that you may come to life. I will put sinews upon you, make flesh grow over you, cover you with skin, and put spirit in you so that you may come to life and know that I am the LORD.

COMMENTARY

Death is God's prescription for our dis-ease. Although most people dread death, it is a release from anxiety and pain. How often do we fear the very thing that will free us?

PRAYER

I'm often anxious for no reason, Lord,
even when things are going well.
Could it be caused
by the tension between what is and what could be?

Thy kingdom come; thy will be done
on earth as it is in heaven.

CANTICLE Canticle of St. Patrick

Evening Prayer

Begin with page 127.

SCRIPTURE *See page 134.*

REFLECTION

Was Christ ever anxious?

PRAYER

In both calm and chaos,
you come to me, Christ,
in either celebration or consolation.
For your presence, I give thanks.

CANTICLE Canticle of Zechariah

Morning Prayer

Begin with page 126.

SCRIPTURE Matthew 23:3b

For they preach but they do not practice.

WORDS OF WISDOM

There once was a woman who was religious and devout and filled with love for God. Each morning she would go to Church. And on her way children would call out to her, beggars would accost her, but so immersed was she in her devotions that she did not even see them.

Now one day she walked down the street in her customary manner and arrived at the church just in time for service. She pushed the door, but it would not open. She pushed it again harder, and found the door was locked.

Distressed at the thought that she would miss service for the first time in years, and not knowing what to do, she looked up. And there, right before her face, was a note pinned to the door.

It said, "I'm out there!" (Anthony de Mello, S.J.)[4]

PRAYER

It's easier to pretend
that I'm not a hypocrite
than to admit my sin
and stand in need of mercy.

Oh, how I like to hold to the illusion
that I have earned your love, Lord.

CANTICLE Canticle of Zechariah

Evening Prayer

Begin with page 127.

SCRIPTURE *See page 136.*

REFLECTION

Is my righteousness keeping me from relating to others?

PRAYER

Even in my hypocrisy
you do not turn your head,
merciful Maker.
In fact, you love my honesty
more than you hate my sin.

CANTICLE Wisdom Canticle

Morning Prayer

Begin with page 126.

SCRIPTURE 1 Peter 3:3-4

Your adornment should not be an external one: braiding the hair, wearing gold jewelry, or dressing in fine clothes, but rather the hidden character of the heart, expressed in the imperishable beauty of a gentle and calm disposition, which is precious in the sight of God.

PUTTING PRAYER INTO PRACTICE

In her quiet and gentle way, St. Monica went about her wifely and motherly duties, praying and putting her faith in God. It took years before her perseverance paid off. Her son, Augustine, after years of sensual gratification, converted to Christianity and became a bishop and a doctor of the Church.

PRAYER

Lord, you who see
the imperishable beauty of the heart,
lead me past vanity and pride
as I strive for a sweet and gentle interior.

CANTICLE Wisdom Canticle

Evening Prayer

Begin with page 127.

SCRIPTURE *See page 138.*

REFLECTION

Is my disposition gentle and calm? If not, what is keeping me from being a calm and gentle person?

PRAYER

Nothing is so strong as gentleness.
Nothing is so gentle as real strength. (St. Francis de Sales)

CANTICLE Canticle of Mary

Morning Prayer

Begin with page 126.

SCRIPTURE Psalm 98:1, 4

Sing to the LORD a new song,
for he has done wondrous deeds;

...Sing joyfully to the LORD, all you lands;
break into song; sing praise.

WORDS OF WISDOM

Every one of us tries to discover how to sing to God. You must sing to him, but you must sing well. He does not want your voice to come harshly to his ears, so sing well, brothers!

If you were asked, "Sing to please this musician," you would not like to do so without having taken some instruction in music, because you would not like to offend an expert in the art. An untrained listener does not notice the faults a musician would point out to you. Who, then, will offer to sing well for God, the great artist whose discrimination is faultless, whose attention is on the minutest detail, whose ear nothing escapes? When will you be able to offer him a perfect performance that you will in no way displease such a supremely discerning listener?

See how he himself provides you with a way of singing. Do not search for words, as if you could find a lyric which would give God pleasure. Sing to him with songs of joy.

This is singing well to God, just singing with songs of joy. (St. Augustine)[5]

PRAYER

With joyful heart and spontaneous spirit,
may I sing today in praise of your creation, Lord!

CANTICLE Canticle of Judith

Evening Prayer

Begin with page 127.

SCRIPTURE *See page 140.*

REFLECTION

What things in life bring me joy?

PRAYER

Fill me with your song.
Open my ears to the celestial symphony
which forever fills the air around me.

CANTICLE Canticle of St. Francis

Morning Prayer

Begin with page 126.

SCRIPTURE John 3:26-30

So they came to John and said to him, "Rabbi, the one who was with you across the Jordan, to whom you testified, here he is baptizing and everyone is coming to him." John answered and said, "No one can receive anything except what has been given him from heaven. You yourselves can testify that I said [that] I am not the Messiah, but that I was sent before him. The one who has the bride is the bridegroom; the best man, who stands and listens for him, rejoices greatly at the bridegroom's voice. So, this joy of mine has been made complete. He must increase; I must decrease."

PUTTING PRAYER INTO PRACTICE

Today, when you find yourself at odds or getting upset, stop and look within. Is some of your distress coming from self-importance?

PRAYER

Lord, give me the vision to see beyond myself
and the humor to laugh at my nearsightedness!

CANTICLE Wisdom Canticle

Evening Prayer

Begin with page 127.

SCRIPTURE John 3:31

The one who comes from above is above all. The one
who is of the earth is earthly and speaks of earthly
things.

REFLECTION

In what ways am I like John the Baptist?

PRAYER

Ah, humility!
How sweet is your company!
You remove the burden of false pride
and lift vanity's veil.

CANTICLE Canticle of Mary

Morning Prayer

Begin with page 126.

SCRIPTURE Matthew 23:25-26

Woe to you, scribes and Pharisees, you hypocrites. You cleanse the outside of cup and dish, but inside they are full of plunder and self-indulgence. Blind Pharisee, cleanse first the inside of the cup, so that the outside also may be clean.

WORDS OF WISDOM

In the initial state of creation, man was made fit for the quiet of contemplation and therefore, "God placed him in a paradise of delights" (Genesis 2:15). But turning from the true light to changeable good, man was bent over by his own fault, and the entire human race by original sin, which infected human nature in two ways: the mind with ignorance and the flesh with concupiscence. As a result, man, blinded and bent over, sits in darkness and does not see the light of heaven unless grace with justice comes to his aid against concupiscence and unless knowledge with wisdom comes to his aid against ignorance. (St. Bonaventure)[6]

PRAYER

> Against the interior enemy
> let me gird myself, O God,
> for only the soul that masters passion
> and confronts illusion
> can journey on to you.

> Glory be to the Father...

CANTICLE Canticle of St. Patrick

Evening Prayer

Begin with page 127.

SCRIPTURE *See page 144.*

REFLECTION

> How can I cleanse my inner self?

PRAYER

> Lead me, Lord, in your path,
> and I will enter into your truth.
> Let my heart rejoice
> that it may fear your name. (Dionysius)

CANTICLE Wisdom Canticle

Morning Prayer

Begin with page 126.

SCRIPTURE 1 Corinthians 15:45-47, 49

So, too, it is written, "The first Adam became a living being," the last Adam a life-giving spirit. But the spiritual was not first; rather the natural and then the spiritual. The first man was from the earth, earthly; the second man, from heaven.... Just as we have borne the image of the earthly one, we shall also bear the image of the heavenly one.

PUTTING PRAYER INTO PRACTICE

Everyone is a wonderful creation, God's handiwork! Try to remember this today as you look into the eyes of a brother or sister.

PRAYER

You are painter, potter, sculptor, composer.
The work of your hand is marvelous to behold.
I praise your name, loving Creator.

CANTICLE Canticle of Mary

Evening Prayer

Begin with page 127.

SCRIPTURE *See page 146.*

REFLECTION

Did I look on anyone today as a miracle of God's creation? Who? What difference did it make in my relationship with that person?

PRAYER

Almighty Artist,
thank you for making me a masterpiece
in the gallery of your universe.

CANTICLE Canticle of St. Francis

Notes

[1] The excerpt from *The Liturgy of the Hours*, copyright ©1975, International Commission on English in the Liturgy, Inc. All rights reserved.

[2] From "That Nature Is a Heraclitean Fire and of the Comfort of the Resurrection" by Gerard Manley Hopkins.

[3] The excerpt from *Fire From Within*, by Carlos Castañeda, copyright ©1984 by Carlos Castañeda and published by Pocket Books, Simon & Schuster, Inc., is reprinted by permission of the author.

[4] The excerpt from *The Prayer of the Frog*, by Anthony de Mello, S.J., copyright ©1988 by Gujarat Sahitta Prakash, Anand, India, is reprinted by permission of the publisher.

[5] The excerpt from *Liturgy of the Hours*, copyright ©1975, International Commission on English in the Liturgy, Inc. All rights reserved.

[6] St. Bonaventure, *The Soul's Journey Into God* (New York: Paulist Press, 1978), p. 62.

September

Opening Song for Morning Prayer

SALUTATION

With joy in my heart, I awake to a universe ablaze with love.

SONG Psalm 136:1-8

Alleluia. Give thanks to the LORD, for he is good,
   for his mercy endures forever.
Give thanks to the God of gods,
   for his mercy endures forever;
Give thanks to the Lord of lords,
   for his mercy endures forever;

Who alone does great wonders,
   for his mercy endures forever;
Who made the heavens in wisdom,
   for his mercy endures forever;
Who spread out the earth upon the waters,
   for his mercy endures forever;
Who made the great lights,
   for his mercy endures forever;
The sun to rule the day
   for his mercy endures forever....

Turn to the page with today's date for the continuation of Morning Prayer.

Opening Song for Evening Prayer

SALUTATION

Come, sweet darkness,
shroud me in the depths
of your mystery.

SONG Psalm 136:9, 10, 16, 23-26

[God made t]he moon and the stars to rule over the
    night;
    for his mercy endures forever;

Who smote the Egyptians in their firstborn,
    for his mercy endures forever;
...Who led his people through the wilderness,
    for his mercy endures forever;
Who remembered us in our abjection,
    for his mercy endures forever;
And freed us from our foes,
    for his mercy endures forever;
Who gives food for all flesh,
    for his mercy endures forever.
Give thanks to the God of heaven,
    for his mercy endures forever.

*Turn to the page with today's date for the continuation of
Evening Prayer.*

Morning Prayer

Begin with page 150.

SCRIPTURE Proverbs 11:1, 26

False scales are an abomination to the LORD,
  but a full weight is his delight....

Him who monopolizes grain, the people curse—
  but blessings upon the head of him who distributes it!

WORDS OF WISDOM

...[W]e must first recall a principle that has always been
taught by the Church: the principle of the priority of
labor over capital.... Since the concept of capital includes
not only the natural resources placed at man's disposal,
but also the whole collection of means by which man
appropriates natural resources and transforms them in
accordance with his needs (and thus in a sense
humanizes them), it must immediately be noted that all
these means are the result of the historical heritage of
human labor.... Thus everything is at the service of
work....

...[L]abor was separated from capital and set in
opposition to it ...as though they were two impersonal
forces....This way of stating the issue contained a
fundamental error, what we can call the error of
economism, that of considering human labor solely
according to its economic purpose....

[M]erely converting the means of production into state
property in the collective systems is by no means

equivalent to socializing that property. We can speak of socializing only when...each person is fully able to consider himself a part-owner of the great workbench at which he is working with everyone else. (John Paul II)[1]

PRAYER

Great Owner of the universe, teach me
    the ways of justice.
Guide my feet in its path; raise my voice in its name.

CANTICLE Canticle of Mary

Evening Prayer

Begin with page 151.

SCRIPTURE *See page 152.*

REFLECTION

In what ways is my money making money for me? Do I see this as separation of capital and labor?

PRAYER

That we all may see the work of our hands and hearts as service rather than drudgery, I pray to you, Lord.
That both employer and employee may cooperate in responsible ways, rather than compete, to promote fairness in the marketplace, I pray to you, Lord.

CANTICLE Canticle of St. Francis

Morning Prayer

Begin with page 150.

SCRIPTURE Matthew 25:21b

Since you were faithful in small matters, I will give you great responsibilities.

PUTTING PRAYER INTO PRACTICE

Do not disregard small duties as unimportant or meaningless. Take as much pride in scrubbing a floor as in organizing a parish committee. Keep this in mind as you perform small tasks today.

PRAYER

Help me to remember, mindful Master,
that it is not the big missions
that accomplish your Kingdom here on earth,
but the small, everyday tasks
that I perform out of love and duty.

CANTICLE Canticle of St. Patrick

Evening Prayer

Begin with page 151.

SCRIPTURE Matthew 25:21b

Since you were faithful in small matters, I will give you
great responsibilities.

REFLECTION

What great responsibilities do I think the Lord would
give me if I were more faithful in small tasks?

PRAYER

You are there with me, Lord,
in the little details of life
as well as the major accomplishments
in my failures as well as my successes.
Even in weakness
when I choose to let my lower nature lead me,
you are there,
waiting for me to call your name.

CANTICLE Canticle of Zechariah

Morning Prayer

Begin with page 150.

SCRIPTURE Luke 4:33-36

In the synagogue, there was a man with the spirit of an unclean demon, and he cried out in a loud voice, "Ha! What have you to do with us, Jesus of Nazareth? Have you come to destroy us? I know who you are—the Holy One of God!" Jesus rebuked him and said, "Be quiet! Come out of him!" Then the demon threw the man down in front of them and came out of him without doing any harm. They were all amazed and said to one another, "What is there about his word? For with authority and power he commands the unclean spirits and they come out."

PUTTING PRAYER INTO PRACTICE

You, too, can dialogue with your demons, so to speak. Is there a fearful figure in your dreams? Is there a part of your shadow side you don't want to look at? These aspects are part of you, to be loved and claimed so that you can reach wholeness. Talk to these isolated parts of your being. Ask them questions. For example, ask the fearful figure in your dream why she or he is trying to scare you, what it is trying to say to you. Dialogue today with the hidden parts of yourself. The communication will help you understand and cope with your fear and shame.

PRAYER

> Holy One,
> help me to touch,
> to embrace
> those parts of me
> that I fear and hate.

CANTICLE Canticle of Mary

Evening Prayer

Begin with page 151.

SCRIPTURE Luke 4:36b

> What is there about his word?

REFLECTION What is there about my own "word" that has power when I dialogue with my shadow side?

PRAYER

> Christ and brother,
> you who are the Word made flesh,
> teach me the power of expression
> which brings the shadow into light.

CANTICLE Canticle of St. Francis

Morning Prayer

Begin with page 150.

SCRIPTURE 1 Corinthians 2:12, 14-16

We have not received the spirit of the world but the Spirit that is from God, so that we may understand the things freely given us by God....

Now the natural person does not accept what pertains to the Spirit of God, for to him it is foolishness, and he cannot understand it, because it is judged spiritually. The spiritual person, however, can judge everything but is not subject to judgment by anyone.

For "who has known the mind of the Lord, so as to counsel him?" But we have the mind of Christ.

PUTTING PRAYER INTO PRACTICE

Be alert today to the areas in your life where you are living as a "natural" man or woman and the areas where you are living as a "spiritual" person.

PRAYER

Lamb of God,
help me to spread my spiritual self
in day-to-day situations
rather than save my spirituality
for Sundays.

CANTICLE Canticle of Zechariah

Evening Prayer

Begin with page 151.

SCRIPTURE 1 Corinthians 2:16b

But we have the mind of Christ.

REFLECTION

Which area in my life would I like to elevate from the natural to the spiritual?

Enter your reflections in your spiritual journal, if you are keeping one.

PRAYER

Creator God,
you have created in me the "mind of Christ"
and I rejoice in the understanding
that comes with this gift.

CANTICLE Canticle of Mary

Morning Prayer

Begin with page 150.

SCRIPTURE Luke 5:7b-9

They came and filled both boats so that they were in danger of sinking. When Simon Peter saw this, he fell at the knees of Jesus and said, "Depart from me, Lord, for I am a sinful man." For astonishment at the catch of fish they had made seized him and all those with him.

PUTTING PRAYER INTO PRACTICE

Strive to work in partnership with the Lord today and you will be astonished at the results. Of course, results are not always visible at once, but when they are, be humble and awed that these fruits came to be through you.

PRAYER

It matters little, Lord,
whether my net is empty or full,
as long as I labor in harmony
with your divine will.

CANTICLE Canticle of St. Patrick

Evening Prayer

Begin with page 151.

SCRIPTURE *See page 160.*

REFLECTION

Do my actions reflect divine integrity?

PRAYER

I cast my net, divine Master,
in your direction,
for you fill it
with all good things.

CANTICLE Canticle of St. Francis

Morning Prayer

Begin with page 150.

SCRIPTURE Luke 5:3b-4, 6, 10b-11

Then he sat down and taught the crowds from the boat. After he had finished speaking, he said to Simon, "Put out into deep water and lower your nets for a catch." ...When they had done this, they caught a great number of fish and their nets were tearing.

Jesus said to Simon, "Do not be afraid; from now on you will be catching men." When they brought their boats to the shore, they left everything and followed him.

PUTTING PRAYER INTO PRACTICE

Be aware of what keeps you from following Christ: the times you are not kind, the times you are critical, and so on.

PRAYER

In a sense,
I leave nothing when I follow you,
because no thing has a value
like the message you bring.
Lamb of God, you are the ultimate reality,
the ground from which all life springs.

CANTICLE Canticle of Judith

Evening Prayer

Begin with page 151.

SCRIPTURE *See page 162.*

REFLECTION

In what ways do I reach out to catch others in a net of love? Do I offend simply because I am unaware of how I come across?

PRAYER

I will fill your net with daily bread
and give your heart
the grace to overcome tribulation,
says the Lord.

CANTICLE Canticle of Zechariah

Morning Prayer

Begin with page 150.

SCRIPTURE Luke 6:12

In those days he departed to the mountain to pray, and he spent the night in prayer to God.

COMMENTARY

Modern life is a flood of sound and activity that threatens to sweep us away. To spend some time in silent meditation is to resist the current, to force it to divide and make its way past us. To meditate in silence is to relax in the hand of God, to let God strip away our tensions and anxieties and bless us with peace.

PRAYER

Though my soul and psyche seek stillness,
my mind, dominated by ego,
feeds on the frenzy of activity.
Free me from the demands of the ego, Lord God,
so that I may think and act
with calmness and clarity.

CANTICLE Wisdom Canticle

Evening Prayer

Begin with page 151.

SCRIPTURE *See page 164.*

REFLECTION

Do I feel wound up? Do I make an effort to turn off the
TV, my worries and my cares? Do I nourish my soul with
silence?

PRAYER

Thus says the Lord:
I who am the infinite source
of energy, wisdom and love
stand waiting to share my power with you.
But alas, you are distracted by trinkets and toys.

CANTICLE Canticle of Mary

Opening Song for Morning Prayer

SALUTATION 2 Samuel 23:3b-4

He that rules over men in justice
   that rules in the fear of God,
is like the morning light of sunrise
   on a cloudless morning
   making the greensward sparkle after rain.

SONG Psalm 146:1-4

Alleluia.
Praise the LORD, O my soul,
   I will praise the LORD all my life;
   I will sing praise to my God while I live.
Put not your trust in princes,
   in man, in whom there is no salvation.
When his spirit departs he returns to his earth;
   on that day his plans perish.

Turn to the page with today's date for the continuation of Morning Prayer.

Opening Song for Evening Prayer

SALUTATION

O God, your glory shines like the sunset
enlightening the horizon!

SONG Psalm 146:5-10

Happy he whose help is the God of Jacob,
   whose hope is in the LORD, his God,
Who made heaven and earth,
   the sea and all that is in them;
Who keeps faith forever,
   secures justice for the oppressed,
   gives food to the hungry.
The LORD sets captives free;
   the LORD gives sight to the blind.
The LORD raises up those that were bowed down;
   the LORD loves the just.
The LORD protects strangers;
   the fatherless and the widow he sustains,
   but the way of the wicked he thwarts.
The LORD shall reign forever—
   your God, O Zion, through all generations. Alleluia.

*Turn to the page with today's date for the continuation of
Evening Prayer.*

Morning Prayer

Begin with page 166.

SCRIPTURE Luke 6:1-2, 5

While he was going through a field of grain on a sabbath, his disciples were picking the heads of grain, rubbing them in their hands, and eating them. Some Pharisees said, "Why are you doing what is unlawful on the sabbath?" ...Then he said to them, "The Son of Man is lord of the sabbath."

PUTTING PRAYER INTO PRACTICE

Think today about how rules keep us from helping and reaching out to one another. Insurance regulations, for example, may prevent us from responding to another's needs.

PRAYER

Free me, Spirit of Truth,
from the mentality of the marketplace
when it sets me at odds
with my brother or sister.

CANTICLE Canticle of St. Patrick

Evening Prayer

Begin with page 167.

SCRIPTURE *See page 168.*

REFLECTION

What is the purpose of each rule or regulation that I
obey? Which ones do I understand and agree with and
which ones do I just follow automatically?

PRAYER

Son of Man,
Lord of the Sabbath,
you remind me that worldly rules
must harmonize with divine authority.
Fortunate are the people
who recognize your reign
and receive your wisdom.

CANTICLE Wisdom Canticle

Morning Prayer

Begin with page 166.

SCRIPTURE Matthew 18:15-17

If your brother sins [against you], go and tell him his
fault between you and him alone. If he listens to you, you
have won over your brother. If he does not listen, take
one or two others along with you, so that "every fact may
be established on the testimony of two or three
witnesses." If he refuses to listen to them, tell the
church. If he refuses to listen even to the church, then
treat him as you would a Gentile or a tax collector.

PUTTING PRAYER INTO PRACTICE

Practice this approach from Matthew when you are at
odds with someone. What a difference it will make in
your relationships! The usual approach is to tell
someone else (often in a gossipy manner) rather than
confront the person who is being accused. Resentment
then begins to build up in the heart of the accuser.

PRAYER

Divine and glorious Healer,
within me there is the sore of stubbornness,
the unwillingness to forgive a hurt
suffered from a loved one.
In my loyalty and love
I needlessly rub the wound with the salt of tears,
unable to leave it alone long enough
to form a healing scab.

CANTICLE Canticle of St. Patrick

Evening Prayer

Begin with page 167.

SCRIPTURE *See page 170.*

REFLECTION

Did someone offend me today? If so, did I go to that person and seek reconciliation before I complained about it to someone else?

PRAYER

Flood my heart with forgiveness,
loving God,
so that I may walk in peace
with my fellow human beings.

CANTICLE Canticle of St. Francis

Morning Prayer

Begin with page 166.

SCRIPTURE Matthew 18:19-20

Again, [amen,] I say to you, if two of you agree on earth about anything for which they are to pray, it shall be granted to them by my heavenly Father. For where two or three are gathered in my name, there am I in the midst of them.

COMMENTARY

What kind of God inspires such words? In pagan legend, gods crave sacrifice, while Greek classics show rivaling deities. The Old Testament even portrays Yahweh's jealousy.

How, then, are we to understand a savior who shares? In a world where rulers rule and leaders lead in order to possess, can mortals be blamed for being suspicious, even doubtful, of the existence of one who pours out his very essence?

Is this why faith is weak and so few pray together in his name?

PUTTING PRAYER INTO PRACTICE

Resolve to pray with one other person at least once a week for a common request. (Do it by phone if you can't do it in person.)

CANTICLE Canticle of Judith

Evening Prayer

Begin with page 167.

SCRIPTURE *See page 172.*

REFLECTION

With whom will I pray this week?

PRAYER

You give me the chance to cocreate
with you and through you.
I sing in praise of your goodness.

CANTICLE Canticle of Mary

Morning Prayer

Begin with page 166.

SCRIPTURE Ezekiel 33:8-9

If I tell the wicked man that he shall surely die, and you do not speak out to dissuade the wicked man from his way, he [the wicked man] shall die for his guilt, but I will hold you responsible for his death. But if you warn the wicked man, trying to turn him from his way, and he refuses to turn from his way, he shall die for his guilt, but you shall save yourself.

PUTTING PRAYER INTO PRACTICE

How often are we silent in the face of wickedness or oppression? If we speak out against injustice, we will not be popular. Going out of our way to get at the truth is a conscious choice. Truth usually does not fall upon us but comes as a result of a search. For example, discovering which political candidate is best for a job requires much investigation—not nearly as much fun as watching TV or reading an adventure novel.

PRAYER

O how difficult, indeed,
to warn the wicked from their ways.
Easier it always is
to avoid their presence
and speak behind their back.
Give me the grace, God,
lovingly to implore another

to turn from the destructiveness of hate.

CANTICLE Canticle of St. Patrick

Evening Prayer

Begin with page 167.

SCRIPTURE *See page 174.*

REFLECTION

Before I warn others of their waywardness, I must practice what I preach. In what ways do hate and fear block my own love for myself, my neighbor and my Creator?

PRAYER

Alone, I can do nothing.
With you, Yahweh, all is possible.

CANTICLE Canticle of Mary

Morning Prayer

Begin with page 166.

SCRIPTURE Luke 6:39b-40

Can a blind person guide a blind person? Will not both fall into a pit? No disciple is superior to the teacher; but when fully trained every disciple will be like his teacher.

MEDITATION EXERCISE

Ira Progoff, in his intensive journal workshops, urges participants to go down into their own private wells where they will reach an underground stream of common sense or inner wisdom. Dialoguing with this core of wisdom is an essential part of the process. To facilitate dialoguing, participants are asked to draw up a list of people, living or dead, who have influenced their lives. They are then encouraged to carry on a written conversation with these significant individuals. It is necessary, in this exercise, to write without thinking, because only then does the participant tap the underground flow of common wisdom. Dialoguing with a frightening dream image, a work problem, a fear or compulsion is also recommended. This technique makes the unknown knowable and renders it harmless. It is a way to tap into our highest self and to nurture that divine seed of wisdom planted in each of us at birth.

PRAYER

Blindly, I grope for the answers
to suffering and injustice,
but like a dream image that has no voice,
I am often ineffective in my efforts to end anguish.

CANTICLE Wisdom Canticle

Evening Prayer

Begin with page 167.

SCRIPTURE *See page 176.*

REFLECTION

Am I willing to discipline myself to find the answers
within?

PRAYER

You give me the opportunity
to make a difference,
to dare to hope and to heal.
You open my eyes
and flood my heart with understanding.
I rest in your compassionate embrace!

CANTICLE Canticle of Zechariah

Morning Prayer

Begin with page 166.

SCRIPTURE Matthew 17:15b-20a

"Lord, have pity on my son, for he is a lunatic and suffers severely; often he falls into fire, and often into water. I brought him to your disciples, but they could not cure him." Jesus said in reply, "O faithless and perverse generation, how long will I be with you? How long will I endure you? Bring him here to me." Jesus rebuked him and the demon came out of him, and from that hour the boy was cured. Then the disciples approached Jesus in private and said, "Why could we not drive it out?" He said to them, "Because of your little faith."

STORY

A man disabled since childhood seriously considered taking a trip to Lourdes. He thought and thought about the possibility of being cured. Convinced that it was possible, he made travel arrangements. But a few weeks before his scheduled departure, he canceled the trip. A friend inquired about his sudden change in plan. "Well," the man responded, "if I went to Lourdes and did not get cured, then I would have wasted my time and money. If I did get cured, however, everyone would expect me to live like a saint the rest of my life. So I decided I would rather keep my handicap."

PRAYER

Healer of my soul, open me up to the divine touch of
healing and grace, so that, at least once today,
I will reach for your strength and attempt to bring
healing and peace to a situation that I normally find
stressful and intolerable.

CANTICLE Canticle of St. Patrick

Evening Prayer

Begin with page 167.

SCRIPTURE *See page 178.*

REFLECTION

In what ways do I choose to remain disabled rather than
accept the responsibility that comes with health of mind
and body?

PRAYER

May the healing power of Christ
restore harmony and peace
to my entire being
as I close my eyes
in blessed slumber.

CANTICLE Canticle of Zechariah

Morning Prayer

Begin with page 166.

SCRIPTURE Luke 6:24-25a

But woe to you who are rich,
for you have received your consolation.
But woe to you who are filled now,
for you will be hungry.

COMMENTARY

This is a Gospel on social justice if ever there was one!
Christ is not talking to millionaires. He's talking to you
and me. Woe to us who are comfortable because we use
more than our share of the world's resources! Woe to us
who dine sumptuously while children in the Third World
starve! Woe to us who aren't willing to risk our
reputations or popularity to speak out against oppression
and prejudice!

PRAYER

Am I well off because I am blessed,
or am I guilty of taking more than my share?
Bestower of all good things, grant me
the understanding and courage to work for justice.

CANTICLE Wisdom Canticle

Evening Prayer

Begin with page 167.

SCRIPTURE *See page 180.*

REFLECTION

What areas of my life are full and overflowing? How do I
share that overflow?

PRAYER

Yahweh, your love is everlasting.
I celebrate the abundance
you pour down upon me
and I am thankful, too,
for the emptiness which leads me
to the "practice of the presence of God."
For it is only in your presence
that I am truly filled
and can proclaim with my ancestors in faith,
"Yahweh, your love is everlasting."

CANTICLE Canticle of Mary

Opening Song for Morning Prayer

SALUTATION Song of Songs 6:10

Who is this that comes forth like the dawn,
as beautiful as the moon, as resplendent as the sun,
as awe-inspiring as bannered troops?

SONG Psalm 127:1-2

Unless the LORD build the house,
they labor in vain who build it.
Unless the LORD guard the city,
in vain does the guard keep vigil.
It is vain for you to rise early,
or put off your rest,
You that eat hard-earned bread,
for he gives to his beloved in sleep.

Turn to the page with today's date for the continuation of Morning Prayer.

Opening Song for Evening Prayer

SALUTATION

> May the peace of night
> descend upon me and my dwelling
> as I await the whisper
> of Yahweh's voice.

SONG Psalm 123:1-4

> To you I lift up my eyes,
>   who are enthroned in heaven.
> Behold, as the eyes of servants
>   are on the hands of their masters,
> As the eyes of a maid
>   are on the hands of her mistress,
> So are our eyes on the LORD, our God,
>   till he have pity on us.
>
> Have pity on us, O LORD, have pity on us,
>   for we are more than sated with contempt;
> Our souls are more than sated
>   with the mockery of the arrogant,
>   with the contempt of the proud.

Turn to the page with today's date for the continuation of Evening Prayer.

Morning Prayer

Begin with page 182.

SCRIPTURE Luke 7:31-35

Then, to what shall I compare the people of this generation? What are they like? They are like children who sit in the marketplace and call to one another,

"We played the flute for you, but you did not dance. We sang a dirge, but you did not weep."

For John the Baptist came neither eating food nor drinking wine, and you said, "He is possessed by a demon." The Son of Man came eating and drinking and you said, "Look, he is a glutton and a drunkard, a friend of tax collectors and sinners." But wisdom is vindicated by all her children.

PUTTING PRAYER INTO PRACTICE

Why is human nature so quick to criticize and so slow to compliment? True generosity of spirit makes another feel valued. Let opportunities to criticize pass you by today. Instead, watch for your chance to make another person feel more valuable.

PRAYER

Divine Spirit, create in me
that ability to sense the specialness,
the individually unique qualities
of every person—including myself.
Relying on your name

and the triumph of the Trinity,
I am confident that I can grow
in generosity of the spirit.

CANTICLE Wisdom Canticle

Evening Prayer

Begin with page 183.

SCRIPTURE *See page 184.*

REFLECTION Do I treat myself with dignity? Do I recognize my
own special uniqueness?

PRAYER

You, Lord, fill me with a sense
of my own personal destiny.
Through you alone,
can I discover and appreciate
who I am.

CANTICLE Canticle of Mary

Morning Prayer

Begin with page 182.

SCRIPTURE 1 Corinthians 3:6-9

I planted, Apollos watered, but God caused the growth.
Therefore, neither the one who plants nor the one who
waters is anything, but only God, who causes the growth.
The one who plants and the one who waters are equal,
and each will receive wages in proportion to his labor.
For we are God's coworkers; you are God's field, God's
building.

WORDS OF WISDOM

When an eight-year-old girl spent her pocket money to
buy her mother a gift, her mother was grateful and
happy, for a mother and house-wife generally gets much
work and little appreciation.

The girl seemed to have understood this for she said,
"It's because you work so hard, mother, and no one
appreciates it."

The woman said, "Your father works hard, too."

Said the girl, "Yes, but he doesn't make a fuss about it."
(Anthony de Mello, S.J.)[2]

PRAYER

My work and efforts, I offer you, Lord God.
Transform my tasks, humble though they are,
into glorious accomplishments
which reflect credit on your holy name!

CANTICLE Canticle of St. Patrick

Evening Prayer

Begin with page 183.

SCRIPTURE *See page 186.*

REFLECTION

Do I lovingly tend the garden plot the Lord has given
me?

PRAYER

I do not toil in vain,
for you, Architect of the universe,
guide my hand and give me direction.
Alleluia!

CANTICLE Canticle of Judith

Morning Prayer

Begin with page 182.

SCRIPTURE Baruch 3:14-15

> Learn where prudence is,
>   where strength, where understanding;
> that you may know also
>   where are length of days, and life,
>   where light of the eyes, and peace.
>
> Who has found the place of wisdom,
>   who has entered into her treasuries?

MEDITATION EXERCISE

> Imagine that you live in a world of abundance where you
> are surrounded with all the resources you need. Imagine
> further that you are incredibly loved, blessed and gifted.
> How would you use your time, treasure and talent to
> serve the Lord? Meditate on the possibilities.

PRAYER

> Lord, open my heart and my eyes
> to the abundance that surrounds me.
> Help me to see my beauty and my gifts.
> Make me aware of the hope buried deep within.
> Give me the daring to step out in faith,
> knowing you will provide all that I need.

CANTICLE Canticle of Mary

Evening Prayer

Begin with page 183.

SCRIPTURE Romans 11:33a

Oh, the depth of the riches and wisdom and knowledge of God!

REFLECTION

How can I take the first step to accomplish my fantasy in this morning's meditation?

PRAYER

Thank you, Lord,
for the unseen gifts
and undeveloped potential
you have bestowed upon me.

CANTICLE Wisdom Canticle

Morning Prayer

Begin with page 182.

SCRIPTURE 1 Corinthians 4:5

Therefore, do not make any judgment before the appointed time, until the Lord comes, for he will bring to light what is hidden in darkness and will manifest the motives of our hearts, and then everyone will receive praise from God.

PUTTING PRAYER INTO PRACTICE

An excuse comes from a subconscious desire to avoid something. When you feel a tugging at the back of your consciousness to do something special for someone like making a phone call, forgiving a slight, smoothing over a misunderstanding or visiting a friend in the hospital, respond to that urge. Do not make excuses. As you develop this gift, you will find yourself responding more and more to the promptings of the Spirit.

PRAYER

Inspired by the Spirit
to do something kind or helpful,
let me not procrastinate, Lord,
for fear that the moment of generosity
will turn into an empty intention.

CANTICLE Canticle of St. Patrick

Evening Prayer

Begin with page 183.

SCRIPTURE 1 Corinthians 4:5b

He will bring to light what is hidden in darkness.

REFLECTION

Did I make any excuses today?

PRAYER

Your integrity is undefiled;
your love, limitless.
How good it is
to live in the house of the Lord.

CANTICLE Canticle of Judith

Morning Prayer

Begin with page 182.

SCRIPTURE John 4:34.

Jesus said to them, "My food is to do the will of the one who sent me and to finish his work."

COMMENTARY

Most of us view doing God's will as demanding and difficult. In actuality, it is the very thing that nourishes us and brings us to fulfillment. In every life there is suffering, but for those who seek to flow with the Spirit, there is seldom despair.

PRAYER

For the freedom from attachment to a personal point of view, a rigid way of doing things that might interfere with accomplishing your will, Lord, I pray.

CANTICLE Canticle of St. Francis

Evening Prayer

Begin with page 183.

SCRIPTURE *See page 192.*

REFLECTION

Do I joyfully strive to "finish God's work" with the attitude that it will make me happy? Or do I think that to live within God's will means giving up the wonderful things in life?

PRAYER

As you were fed and nourished by the Father,
Brother Jesus,
so too are we sustained by your words and example.

CANTICLE Canticle of Zechariah

Morning Prayer

Begin with page 182.

SCRIPTURE John 4:35b-38

I tell you, look up and see the fields ripe for the harvest. The reaper is already gathering crops for eternal life, so that the sower and reaper can rejoice together. For here the saying is verified that "One sows and another reaps." I sent you to reap what you have not worked for; others have done the work, and you are sharing the fruits of their work.

PUTTING PRAYER INTO PRACTICE

Many people believe that they have earned or deserve everything they have. Christ encourages hard work, but he also wants us to recognize that we often reap where others have sown. See the land you now occupy, the life-style you enjoy. Think about all those who went before you to make it all possible.

PRAYER

I am indeed blessed
by the beauty of the souls around me—
those precious presences whom Divine Providence
has provided without price.

CANTICLE Canticle of Judith

Evening Prayer

Begin with page 183.

SCRIPTURE John 4:37b

One sows and another reaps.

REFLECTION

In what ways am I sharing in the fruits of another's work?

PRAYER

May I grow in gratefulness
for that steady stream of humanity that preceded me,
preparing the place in which I now prosper.

CANTICLE Canticle of St. Francis

Morning Prayer

Begin with page 182.

SCRIPTURE Luke 6:35-36

But rather, love your enemies and do good to them, and lend expecting nothing back; then your reward will be great and you will be children of the Most High, for he himself is kind to the ungrateful and the wicked. Be merciful just as [also] your Father is merciful.

PUTTING PRAYER INTO PRACTICE

As Christians, we are often kind and helpful to those whom we consider "deserving." But how often do we reach out to help, or welcome into our midst, the ungrateful? Today, reach out in kindness to someone that you perceive as "undeserving." Lend money and expect no return.

PRAYER

Keep me from judging
and shunning those I consider unworthy.
Give me your goodness,
generous God,
so that I can be compassionate
even to those who annoy me.

CANTICLE Canticle of St. Patrick

Evening Prayer

Begin with page 183.

SCRIPTURE *See page 196.*

REFLECTION

In what way today did I live what Christ was asking in today's Scripture selection?

PRAYER

Brother Jesus!
Without your words
and your example,
mercy would be unknown.

Glory be to the Father....

CANTICLE Canticle of Zechariah

Opening Song for Morning Prayer

SALUTATION

> Give ear, O heavens, while I speak;
>> let the earth hearken to the words of my mouth!
>
> May my instruction soak in like the rain,
>> and my discourse permeate like the dew,
>
> Like a downpour upon the grass,
>> like a shower upon the crops:
>
> For I will sing the LORD's renown.
> Oh, proclaim the greatness of our God!
> (Deuteronomy 32:1-3)

SONG Psalm 103:8-11

> Merciful and gracious is the LORD,
>> slow to anger and abounding in kindness.
>
> He will not always chide,
>> nor does he keep his wrath forever.
>
> Not according to our sins does he deal with us,
>> nor does he requite us according to our crimes.
>
> For as the heavens are high above the earth,
> so surpassing is his kindness toward those who fear him.

Turn to the page with today's date for the continuation of Morning Prayer.

Opening Song for Evening Prayer

SALUTATION

Oh, how the wonder of the evening
returns my thoughts to you,
Eternal Friend and Divine Lover!

SONG Psalm 103:12-17a

As far as the east is from the west,
 so far has he put our transgressions from us.
As a father has compassion on his children,
 so the LORD has compassion on those who fear him,
For he knows how we are formed;
 he remembers that we are dust.
Man's days are like those of grass;
 like a flower of the field he blooms;
The wind sweeps over him and he is gone,
 and his place knows him no more.
But the kindness of the LORD is from eternity
 to eternity toward those who fear him....

*Turn to the page with today's date for the continuation of
Evening Prayer.*

Morning Prayer

Begin with page 198.

SCRIPTURE Luke 19:5b-6, 9-10

> Jesus looked up and said to him, "Zacchaeus, come down quickly, for today I must stay at your house." And he came down quickly and received him with joy.... And Jesus said to him, "Today salvation has come to this house because this man too is a descendant of Abraham. For the Son of Man has come to seek and to save what was lost."

PUTTING PRAYER INTO PRACTICE

Jesus invites himself into the home of a despicable sinner—a tax collector. Today, be hospitable to someone whom society rejects.

PRAYER

Touch me, Jesus. Mend my brokenness and make me whole.

CANTICLE Canticle of Mary

Evening Prayer

Begin with page 199.

SCRIPTURE *See page 200.*

REFLECTION

Did I reach out today to someone whom my culture considers inferior? What barriers stop me from doing this more often—my need for cleanliness, hygiene or order? My pride or my concern for what others think?

PRAYER

Oh, lucky the person
who has the humility of Zacchaeus!
For such a one receives Christ
in his or her heart.

CANTICLE Canticle of St. Francis

Morning Prayer

Begin with page 198.

SCRIPTURE Luke 6:43, 45

A good tree does not bear rotten fruit, nor does a rotten tree bear good fruit.... A good person out of the store of goodness in his heart produces good, but an evil person out of a store of evil produces evil; for from the fullness of the heart the mouth speaks.

PUTTING PRAYER INTO PRACTICE

Listen to yourself today. Pay close attention to your own words, your expressions while speaking. This is the way to wisdom, for you will learn what is in your own heart.

PRAYER

Like a beautiful fruit tree,
grounded in the word of truth
and nourished by living waters,
may I too bear wholesome fruit.

CANTICLE Canticle of Mary

Evening Prayer

Begin with page 199.

SCRIPTURE *See page 202.*

REFLECTION

What did I discover when I listened to my own words?

PRAYER

Gardener of my soul,
you teach me
how to replace thorns
with roses.

Say the Hail Mary ten times, all the while thinking about the roses blooming within your being.

CANTICLE Canticle of Mary

Morning Prayer

Begin with page 198.

SCRIPTURE Luke 8:5-8

"A sower went out to sow his seed. And as he sowed, some seed fell on the path and was trampled, and the birds of the sky ate it up. Some seed fell on rocky ground, and when it grew, it withered for lack of moisture. Some seed fell among thorns, and the thorns grew with it and choked it. And some seed fell on good soil, and when it grew, it produced fruit a hundred-fold." After saying this, he called out, "Whoever has ears to hear ought to hear."

MEDITATION EXERCISE

Examine your motives today. How deep is your faith and what does it mean? Do you seek after goodness to get to heaven? Do you treat people kindly only when they reciprocate, or do you act out of kindness because you are convinced that is how you want to act regardless of the other person's behavior?

PRAYER

In the aftermath
of a fresh conversion or mystical encounter,
it is easy to love you, Lord.
But as the newness wears off,
as the sense of adventure
dissolves into daily duty,
let me then shine

with the spirituality of perseverance!

CANTICLE Canticle of St. Patrick

Evening Prayer

Begin with page 199.

SCRIPTURE *See page 204.*

REFLECTION

How conscientious am I in my work and in my
relationships? How can I cultivate the soil in my soul?

PRAYER

Thank you, Heavenly Creator,
for the potential that you plant
and the power that you place in me
to become my best.

CANTICLE Canticle of Mary

Morning Prayer

Begin with page 198.

SCRIPTURE Proverbs 30:7-9

> Two things I ask of you,
>   deny them not to me before I die:
> Put falsehood and lying far from me,
>   give me neither poverty nor riches;
>   [provide me only with the food I need];
> Lest, being full, I deny you,
>   saying, "Who is the Lord?"
> Or, being in want, I steal,
>   and profane the name of my God.

COMMENTARY

Success may be usually more detrimental to a person's character than failure. With failure, we may learn and grow, provided we are not so desperate that we turn to crime. With success, we may become egotistical and acquire a false sense of security because of our wealth or status.

PRAYER

Keep me from the desire for riches, Lord.
Give me the wisdom to see that most of my needs
are really wants in disguise.
Protect me from poverty, too,
so that in desperation I do not
turn to theft for my daily bread.

CANTICLE Wisdom Canticle

Evening Prayer

Begin with page 199.

SCRIPTURE *See page 206.*

REFLECTION

For what riches (fame, power, popularity, beauty, wealth) do I secretly long?

PRAYER

Your wisdom, wise God, is my wealth,
and your love is my reason for living.
Joyfully, I proclaim your goodness!

CANTICLE Canticle of Judith

Morning Prayer

Begin with page 198.

SCRIPTURE Luke 8:21b

My mother and my brothers are those who hear the
word of God and act on it.

COMMENTARY

When you ground your relationships in virtues such as
honesty, patience and service, you form community with
the family of God.

PRAYER

Enable me, Lord,
to build friendships based on ideals
that transcend earthly, worldly realities.

CANTICLE Canticle of St. Patrick

Evening Prayer

Begin with page 199.

SCRIPTURE Luke 8:21b

My mother and my brothers are those who hear the word of God and act on it.

REFLECTION

In my relationships, how often do I seek to get love rather than give love?

PRAYER

Brother Jesus,
you remind us that spiritual bonds
are more important than bloodlines
to those who hear the Word of God
and acknowledge him as Savior.

CANTICLE Canticle of Zechariah

September 27

Morning Prayer

Begin with page 198.

SCRIPTURE Luke 9:22, 44-45

[Jesus] said, "The Son of Man must suffer greatly and be rejected by the elders, the chief priests, and the scribes, and be killed and on the third day be raised.

"...Pay attention to what I am telling you. The Son of Man is to be handed over to men." But they did not understand this saying; its meaning was hidden from them so that they should not understand it, and they were afraid to ask him about this saying.

COMMENTARY

There is no such thing as needless suffering—it is all redemptive as long as we place ourselves under God's will. That does not mean that we go out and look for suffering but, rather, that we look for God's will and take the suffering that comes with it in our stride.

PRAYER

You show us,
Son of Man,
that rejection and suffering
are part of every life,
for the material realm
by its very essence
is bound by limitations,
while our spiritual side

seeks growth and endless discovery
of your infinite mystery.

CANTICLE Canticle of Zechariah

Evening Prayer

Begin with page 199.

SCRIPTURE *See page 210.*

REFLECTION

Some of my suffering comes from selfishness and some
of it comes as a natural consequence of my bodily
limitations. Can I tell which is which?

PRAYER

Christ, you give me the strength to carry my cross and
the wisdom to discern which cross is mine.

CANTICLE Canticle of Mary

Morning Prayer

Begin with page 198.

SCRIPTURE Zechariah 2:9, 14

But I will be for her [Jerusalem] an encircling wall of fire, says the LORD, and I will be the glory in her midst.

...Sing and rejoice, O daughter Zion! See, I am coming to dwell among you, says the LORD.

PUTTING PRAYER INTO PRACTICE

Often we are too absorbed in our own pursuit of happiness to be sensitive to the happiness of others. Be aware today when you fail to be considerate of others simply because you are so busy with your own agenda.

PRAYER

Into the midst of my daily existence,
I invite you, Lord of hosts:
into the struggle to survive,
the pursuit of pleasure
and the escapes from pain.
In your arms
I place my fragmented psyche
and my conscience, tormented by guilt.
Ease my anxiety and forgive my trespasses,
even when I run
from the embrace of your penetrating love.

CANTICLE Canticle of Judith

Evening Prayer

Begin with page 199.

SCRIPTURE *See page 212.*

REFLECTION

Do I realize how often I wound others, unknowingly,
simply because I refuse to look at myself as others see
me?

PRAYER

You live in our midst, Lord,
when we, your sons and daughters,
affirm and care for one another.

CANTICLE Canticle of Zechariah

Morning Prayer

Begin with page 198.

SCRIPTURE Luke 9:60b

Let the dead bury their dead. But you, go and proclaim
the Kingdom of God.

PUTTING PRAYER INTO PRACTICE

Notice the times today when you feel dead or stale,
without spark or passion. Invite the Holy Spirit into the
moment.

PRAYER

Slowly, almost imperceptibly,
the Spirit, invited,
enters into the mortal realm,
blessing one's daily toil with dignity
and one's personal encounters with trust.

CANTICLE Canticle of St. Patrick

Evening Prayer

Begin with page 199.

SCRIPTURE Luke 9:60b

Let the dead bury their dead. But you, go and proclaim the Kingdom of God.

REFLECTION

What difference did it make, in the events of my life today, when I invited the Holy Spirit into the moment?

PRAYER

You give vitality to my being
and bring concentration to my doing.
I praise your presence, Spirit Divine!

CANTICLE Wisdom Canticle

Morning Prayer

Begin with page 198.

SCRIPTURE Philippians 2:13-16

For God is the one who, for his good purpose, works in you both to desire and to work. Do everything without grumbling or questioning, that you may be blameless and innocent, children of God without blemish in the midst of a crooked and perverse generation, among whom you shine like lights in the world, as you hold on to the word of life, so that my boast for the day of Christ may be that I did not run in vain or labor in vain.

PUTTING PRAYER INTO PRACTICE

I am convinced that one of the reasons the kingdom of God is not built faster on this earth is because the "laborers in the vineyards" want job descriptions. Few people are willing to suffer the discomfort that goes with working without clarity and structure. Yet God gives us the creativity and abilities to move out of the system (which is often wicked and perverse with its emphasis on efficiency and profit). Today, employ all of your God-given talents to discover more loving and humane ways of dealing with conflict.

PRAYER

How sad it is that,
although we are invited to a royal banquet
we prefer to stand like beggars,
knocking at the gate for a crust of bread.

CANTICLE Canticle of Zechariah

Evening Prayer

Begin with page 199.

SCRIPTURE *See page 216.*

REFLECTION

How can I be more creative and innovative in showing love and compassion to the people I come into contact with in my day-to-day existence?

PRAYER

It is amazing what you, God, can do
through a person who doesn't care who gets the credit.
(Author unknown)

CANTICLE Canticle of Mary

Notes

[1] The excerpt from *Laborem Exercens* (1981), #12-14, was taken from *Justice in the Marketplace*, National Conference of Catholic Bishops/United States Catholic Conference, copyright ©1985, and is used with permission.

[2] The excerpt from *The Prayer of the Frog*, by Anthony de Mello, S.J., copyright ©1988 by Gujarat Sahitta Prakash, Anand, India, is reprinted by permission of the publisher.

October

Opening Song for Morning Prayer

SALUTATION

Messenger of the morning!
You bring hope and energy
to the dawn of each new day!

SONG Psalm 147:1-6

Praise the LORD, for he is good;
    sing praise to our God, for he is gracious;
    it is fitting to praise him.
The LORD rebuilds Jerusalem,
    the dispersed of Israel he gathers.
He heals the brokenhearted
    and binds up their wounds.
He tells the number of the stars;
    he calls them each by name.
Great is our Lord and mighty in power:
    to his wisdom there is no limit.
The LORD sustains the lowly;
    the wicked he casts to the ground.

Turn to the page with today's date for the continuation of Morning Prayer.

Opening Song for Evening Prayer

SALUTATION

Rejoice, O my soul,
and greet the evening with gladness!

SONG Psalm 147:12-18

Glorify the LORD, O Jerusalem;
  praise your God, O Zion.
For God has strengthened the bars of your gates;
  he has blessed your children within you.
He has granted peace in your borders;
  with the best of wheat he fills you.
He sends forth his command to the earth;
  swiftly runs his word!
He spreads snow like wool;
  frost he strews like ashes.
He scatters his hail like crumbs;
  before his cold the waters freeze.
He sends his word and melts them;
  he lets his breeze blow and the waters run.

Turn to the page with today's date for the continuation of Evening Prayer.

Morning Prayer

Begin with page 220.

SCRIPTURE Matthew 17:20b

Amen, I say to you, if you have faith the size of a mustard seed, you will say to this mountain, "Move from here to there," and it will move. Nothing will be impossible for you.

PUTTING PRAYER INTO PRACTICE

Today look for the good or the positive in every person and situation. Bring Christ's strength within you to every happening so that even where there is suffering, all things can work for the good. This works even for an event which is over and done, such as an automobile accident. Ask yourself why it happened, what caused it and what lesson is to be learned from it.

PRAYER

May I put on Christ's strength,
so that I might become
a calm, positive influence
in the midst of hurt, despair or chaos.

CANTICLE Wisdom Canticle

Evening Prayer

Begin with page 221.

SCRIPTURE *See page 222.*

REFLECTION

What situation did I transform from a negative to a positive experience? How did I do it?

Enter your reflections in your spiritual journal, if you are keeping one. Describe your emotional response to the situation and describe in detail how you were able to focus positive emotional energy in the situation.

PRAYER

For your ending prayer today, think of all the wonderful, good things in your life. As you think of one, pray gratefully to the Lord before going on to the next one. Think of those experiences in your life that you perceived as "bad" but that turned out to nurture growth and be life-giving. Pray in gratitude for these experiences.

CANTICLE Canticle of Judith

Morning Prayer

Begin with page 220.

SCRIPTURE Acts 12:6b-9, 11ab

...Peter, secured by double chains, was sleeping between two soldiers, while outside the door guards kept watch on the prison. Suddenly, the angel of the Lord stood by him and a light shone in the cell. He tapped Peter on the side and awakened him, saying, "Get up quickly." The chains fell from his wrists. The angel said to him, "Put on your belt and your sandals." He did so. Then he said to him, "Put on your cloak and follow me." So he followed him out, not realizing that what was happening through the angel was real; he thought he was seeing a vision.... Then he recovered his senses and said, "Now I know for certain that [the] Lord sent his angel and rescued me...."

WORDS OF WISDOM

When, by force of death, [the soul] is snatched from the weight of the flesh that closed it in, it trembles with excitement to see the face of the angel, the summoner of souls, realizing that its eternal abode has been prepared. (Tertullian)[1]

PRAYER

Earth's crammed with heaven,
And every common bush afire with God;
But only he who sees takes off his shoes;
The rest sit round it and pluck blackberries. (Elizabeth Barrett Browning)[2]

CANTICLE Canticle of St. Francis

Evening Prayer

Begin with page 221.

SCRIPTURE Acts 13:11b

Now I know for certain that the Lord sent his angel and rescued me.

REFLECTION

In a sense, my guardian angel is my own personal spiritual director. How can I open up and become more aware of this voice and vision in my life?

PRAYER

Guardian and guide,
so steeped am I in my own material reality
that I am often unaware
of your spirit around me.
Thank you, angel and messenger,
for your constant intercession.
Help me to hear your whisperings
and seek your direction.
I bow humbly in gratitude
for your presence and protection.

CANTICLE Canticle of Zechariah

Morning Prayer

Begin with page 220.

SCRIPTURE Philippians 1:21-24

For to me, life is Christ, and death is gain. If I go on living in the flesh, that means fruitful labor for me. And I do not know which I shall choose. I am caught between the two. I long to depart this life and be with Christ, [for] that is far better. Yet that I remain [in] the flesh is more necessary for your benefit.

WORDS OF WISDOM

Now, the source of all evil is the desire to possess. Mindful that we brought nothing into this world and can take nothing out of it, let us put on the armor of righteousness. (St. Polycarp)

PRAYER

Free me, God,
from the compulsion to control
and the passion to possess.

CANTICLE Canticle of St. Patrick

Evening Prayer

Begin with page 221.

SCRIPTURE *See page 226.*

REFLECTION

At what times today was I aware of my desire to possess or control?

PRAYER

O, how my spirit longs
to step out of this suit of skin
and slip into eternity!

CANTICLE Wisdom Canticle

Morning Prayer

Begin with page 220.

SCRIPTURE Matthew 10:7-10

As you go, make this proclamation: "The kingdom of heaven is at hand." Cure the sick, raise the dead, cleanse lepers, drive out demons. Without cost you have received; without cost you are to give. Do not take gold or silver or copper for your belts; no sack for the journey, or a second tunic, or sandals, or walking stick. The laborer deserves his keep.

WORDS OF WISDOM

Our Lord...tells us, *Love your enemies, do good to those who hate you* (Luke 6:27). We are bound to order our lives according to the precepts and counsels of our Lord Jesus Christ, and so we must renounce self and bring our lower nature into subjection under the yoke of obedience; this is what we have all promised God....

It is not for us to be wise and calculating in the world's fashion; we should be guileless, lowly, and pure.... We should not want to be in charge of others; we are to be servants, and should *be subject to every human creature for God's sake* (1 Peter 2:13). On all those who do this and endure to the last the Spirit of God will rest (cf. Isaiah 11:2); he will make his dwelling in them and there he will stay, and they will be *children of your Father in heaven* (Matthew 5:45) whose work they do. It is they who are the brides, the brothers and the mothers of our Lord

Jesus Christ. (St. Francis of Assisi, "Letter to All the Faithful")[3]

PRAYER

Compassionate and tender God,
guide my feet into the way of peace.
Give me a patient and steadfast heart,
willing to make the sacrifices necessary
to live in harmony with all people.

CANTICLE Canticle of St. Francis

Evening Prayer

Begin with page 221.

SCRIPTURE *See page 228.*

REFLECTION

Whom did I serve today?

PRAYER

For the beauty of your son, St. Francis,
and the grace of his stark simplicity,
I sing and shout for joy!

CANTICLE Canticle of Judith

Morning Prayer

Begin with page 220.

SCRIPTURE Nehemiah 8:9b-10

"Today is holy to the LORD your God. Do not be sad, and do not weep"—for all the people were weeping as they heard the words of the law. He said further: "Go, eat rich foods and drink sweet drinks, and allot portions to those who had nothing prepared; for today is holy to our LORD. Do not be saddened this day, for rejoicing in the Lord must be your strength."

PUTTING PRAYER INTO PRACTICE

Abraham Lincoln once said that people are just about as happy as they make up their minds to be. Make up your mind to be happy. Brighten someone's day.

PRAYER

Help me to understand,
wise and loving God,
that happiness is not a matter of circumstance
but a result of personal integrity.

CANTICLE Wisdom Canticle

Evening Prayer

Begin with page 221.

SCRIPTURE *See page 230.*

REFLECTION

Was my day rooted in joy and did that joy carry me over
the rough spots? If not, why?

PRAYER

Creator of the Cosmos,
you give me the inner wisdom
to see order and beauty,
to hear rhythm and melody,
to feel harmony and love
in the unfolding scheme of things.
Confident that all consciousness
is struggling to fulfill your wondrous will,
my heart takes delight in the divine destiny.

CANTICLE Canticle of Zechariah

Morning Prayer

Begin with page 220.

SCRIPTURE John 13:34-35

I give you a new commandment: love one another. As I have loved you, so you also should love one another. This is how all will know that you are my disciples, if you have love for one another.

PUTTING PRAYER INTO PRACTICE

Love is attention. What gets your attention? Where do you put your time? What thoughts are you preoccupied with as you go about your daily duties? Remember that the greatest gift we can give one another is our full attention. Practice this in your relationships today.

PRAYER

Gift me, God,
with moments of rich concentration.
Guide my thoughts so that I can give
my rapt attention to those I meet today.

CANTICLE Canticle of St. Patrick

Evening Prayer

Begin with page 221.

SCRIPTURE *See page 232.*

REFLECTION

What cares and concerns kept me from giving the person
or task at hand my rapt attention?

PRAYER

In thanksgiving
for those times in my life, Lord,
when my mind and heart sing
in the spirit of pure communion,
I pray to you,
Creator God.

CANTICLE Canticle of St. Francis

Morning Prayer

Begin with page 220.

SCRIPTURE 1 Samuel 13:13-14

Samuel's response [to King Saul] was: "You have been foolish! Had you kept the command the LORD your God gave you, the LORD would now establish your kingship in Israel as lasting; but as things are, your kingdom shall not endure. The LORD has sought out a man after his own heart and has appointed him commander of his people, because you broke the LORD's command."

PUTTING PRAYER INTO PRACTICE

Do not put your trust in technology; it will enslave you in its iron arms. Nor can your investments free you from need. In justice and truth alone comes liberation from the cycle of toil and pain. Trust in the God who is Love.

PRAYER

You alone,
O God of justice and truth,
Speak the words of life.
I listen for your voice.

CANTICLE Wisdom Canticle

Evening Prayer

Begin with page 221.

SCRIPTURE *See page 234.*

REFLECTION

In what ways do I break the Lord's command by seeking my own way?

PRAYER

Sit in silent meditation, seeking the answer to the above question.

CANTICLE Canticle of Mary

Opening Song for Morning Prayer

SALUTATION

The morning light shines around me. Yet how often its splendor goes unnoticed!

SONG Psalm 26:1-7

Do me justice, O LORD! for I have walked in integrity,
    and in the LORD I trust without wavering.
Search me, O LORD, and try me;
    test my soul and my heart.

For your kindness is before my eyes,
    and I walk in your truth.
I stay not with worthless men,
    nor do I consort with hypocrites.
I hate the assembly of evildoers,
    and with the wicked I will not stay.
I wash my hands in innocence,
    and I go around your altar, O LORD,
Giving voice to my thanks
    and recounting all your wondrous deeds.

Turn to the page with today's date for the continuation of Morning Prayer.

Opening Song for Evening Prayer

SALUTATION

Calm is the night, O Lord, as I wait for you.

SONG Psalm 26:8-12

O Lord, I love the house in which you dwell,
the tenting-place of your glory.

Gather not my soul with those of sinners.
nor with men of blood my life.
On their hands are crimes,
and their right hands are full of bribes.
But I walk in integrity;
redeem me, and have pity on me.
My foot stands on level ground;
in the assemblies I will bless the LORD.

Turn to the page with today's date for the continuation of Evening Prayer.

Morning Prayer

Begin with page 236.

SCRIPTURE Psalm 61:5

Oh, that I might lodge in your tent forever,
take refuge in the shelter of your wings!

WORDS OF WISDOM

Man was made in the image and likeness of God; in
image he possesses freedom of will, and in likeness he
possesses virtues. The likeness has been destroyed;
however, man conserves the image. The image can be
burned in hell but not consumed. It is damaged but not
destroyed. Through fate as such it is not effaced, but
subsists. Wherever the soul is, there also will be the
image. It is not so with the likeness. This remains in the
soul which accomplishes the good; in the soul which sins
it is wretchedly transformed. The soul which has sinned
ranks with beasts devoid of intelligence. (St. Bernard of
Clairvaux)[4]

PRAYER

You, who are the Originator,
the Source of energy and love,
whose being overflows,
giving life and force to angelic form
for the purpose of guiding souls
back to your likeness:
I laugh and rejoice in you,
Designer and Creator.

CANTICLE Canticle of Judith

Evening Prayer

Begin with page 237.

SCRIPTURE *See page 238.*

REFLECTION

How can I nurture the "good likeness"?

Enter your reflections in your spiritual journal, if you are keeping one.

PRAYER

You, God, are the center,
the focus, the force and essence of all life.
Unnameable, unknowable
Maker of All,
I come to you in awe!

CANTICLE Wisdom Canticle

Morning Prayer

Begin with page 236.

SCRIPTURE Luke 10:38-42

As they continued their journey [Jesus] entered a village where a woman whose name was Martha welcomed him. She had a sister named Mary [who] sat beside the Lord at his feet listening to him speak. Martha, burdened with much serving, came to him and said, "Lord, do you not care that my sister has left me by myself to do the serving? Tell her to help me." The Lord said to her in reply, "Martha, Martha, you are anxious and worried about many things. There is need of only one thing. Mary has chosen the better part and it will not be taken from her."

PUTTING PRAYER INTO PRACTICE

As you go about your daily activity, notice when you get anxious and worried. Stop the cycle of hurried activity or hurried thoughts that is driving you. Choose to remember that God makes all things well. Choose to enjoy the moment and the task at hand. As a child of God, let your actions come out of the calm center of your being, which is connected to the Creator.

PRAYER

> Loving God,
> don't let me fret my time away
> feeling guilty about the past
> or anxious about the future.
> Let me instead say yes joyfully
> to whatever the moment may bring.

CANTICLE Canticle of Mary

Evening Prayer

Begin with page 237.

SCRIPTURE *See page 240.*

REFLECTION

> Are my actions and choices fruits of my reflection and
> prayer life?

PRAYER

> Thank you, Brother Jesus,
> for reminding me
> that there is a better way
> if only I choose to take it.

CANTICLE Canticle of Zechariah

Morning Prayer

Begin with page 236.

SCRIPTURE Judges 13:3-5, 24

> An angel of the LORD appeared to the woman and said to her, "Though you are barren and have had no children, yet you will conceive and bear a son. Now, then, be careful to take no wine or strong drink and to eat nothing unclean. As for the son you will conceive and bear, no razor shall touch his head, for the boy is to be consecrated to God from the womb. It is he who will begin the deliverance of Israel from the power of the Philistines...."

> The woman bore a son and named him Samson.

PUTTING PRAYER INTO PRACTICE

> By inheritance and image, we are children of God; by temperament and inclination, we are children of the earth. And the best and worst of life comes from attempts to reconcile these two apparently conflicting influences. Be aware today of when these two influences clash and when they harmonize.

PRAYER

> Lord of Creation,
> be with me as I struggle
> with the limitations of my senses
> and the difficulties inherent
> in being a child of the earth.

CANTICLE Canticle of Mary

Evening Prayer

Begin with page 237.

SCRIPTURE *See page 242.*

REFLECTION

At what times today did I strive to synthesize worldly
values with spiritual values?

PRAYER

Glorious God,
I cherish your guidance and protection
as I journey along the natural and supernatural paths
which lead me home to you.

CANTICLE Wisdom Canticle

Morning Prayer

Begin with page 236.

SCRIPTURE 1 Timothy 4:1-4

Now the Spirit explicitly says that in the last times some
will turn away from the faith by paying attention to
deceitful spirits and demonic instructions through the
hypocrisy of liars with branded consciences. They forbid
marriage and require abstinence from foods that God
created to be received with thanksgiving by those who
believe and know the truth. For everything created by
God is good, and nothing is to be rejected when received
with thanksgiving....

PUTTING PRAYER INTO PRACTICE

Meister Eckhart says that God enjoys himself and all
creatures. The same is true for us. The more we see God
in all things, including ourself, the more we can enjoy
God in all things. True thanksgiving is enjoyment.

PRAYER

All of creation is a blessing,
and I am one of its marvels!
Help me to understand my uniqueness, Father,
and claim my birthright as your child.

CANTICLE Canticle of Mary

Evening Prayer

Begin with page 237.

SCRIPTURE *See page 244.*

REFLECTION What people or activities did I enjoy today? How can I increase my capacity for enjoyment?

PRAYER

Creator of all,
it is only when I can enjoy your creation
that I am truly grateful.
Give me the grace to see you in all things.

CANTICLE Canticle of St. Francis

Morning Prayer

Begin with page 236.

Begin with page 236.

SCRIPTURE Ephesians 1:3-10

Blessed be the God and Father of our Lord Jesus Christ, who has blessed us in Christ with every spiritual blessing in the heavens, as he chose us in him, before the foundation of the world, to be holy and without blemish before him. In love he destined us for adoption to himself through Jesus Christ, in accord with the favor of his will, for the praise of the glory of his grace that he granted us in the beloved.

In him we have redemption by his blood, the forgiveness of transgression, in accord with the riches of his grace that he lavished upon us. In all wisdom and insight, he has made known to us the mystery of his will in accord with his favor that he set forth in him as a plan for the fullness of times, to sum up all things in Christ, in heaven and on earth.

REFLECTION

Consider the implications of being God's adopted— chosen—child. What difference will that make in your actions today? How will you reflect the divine love to others?

PRAYER

The mystery of your plans
unraveling in time,

is known only to the mind
enlightened by divine insight.

CANTICLE Canticle of Zechariah

Evening Prayer

Begin with page 237.

SCRIPTURE *See page 246.*

REFLECTION

What state of mind was I in today when my actions
reflected divine love?

*Enter your reflections in your spiritual journal, if you are
keeping one.*

PRAYER

Lord, I am unworthy of your love
and your generosity, which knows no bounds.
I play as a child at your feet,
hoping to glimpse the divine countenance.

CANTICLE Wisdom Canticle

Morning Prayer

Begin with page 236.

SCRIPTURE 1 Timothy 6:6-9

Indeed, religion with contentment is a great gain. For we brought nothing into the world, just as we shall not be able to take anything out of it. If we have food and clothing, we shall be content with that. Those who want to be rich are falling into temptation and into a trap and into many foolish and harmful desires, which plunge them into ruin and destruction.

PUTTING PRAYER INTO PRACTICE

Succoth, from a Hebrew word meaning "tents," is a Jewish thanksgiving festival that begins in October with the harvest moon. Small temporary shelters of foliage, flowers and fruit provide sleeping quarters for the men harvesting in the fields. In our temporary stay on earth, we would be wise to imitate the harvesters—leaving security and comfort behind in order to reap the harvest.

PRAYER

The more I embrace emptiness
and become content with sufficiency,
the more my spirit soars to fulfillment,
Lord God,
bestower of all good things!

CANTICLE Canticle of Judith

Evening Prayer

Begin with page 237.

SCRIPTURE *See page 248.*

REFLECTION

Are my needs for security standing in my way of leading a full life? Are security needs stopping me from being myself?

PRAYER

Father, I thank you for my daily bread.
Bless the harvest and the work of my hands.
May I be content with sufficiency and not covet riches.
In gratitude I pray the prayer your Son gave us:

Our Father....

CANTICLE Canticle of Zechariah

Morning Prayer

Begin with page 236.

SCRIPTURE John 14:1-6a

"Do not let your hearts be troubled. You have faith in God; have faith also in me. In my Father's house there are many dwelling places. If there were not, would I have told you that I am going to prepare a place for you? And if I go and prepare a place for you, I will come back again and take you to myself, so that where I am you also may be. Where [I] am going you know the way." Thomas said to him, "Master, we do not know where you are going; how can we know the way?" Jesus said to him, "I am the way, the truth and the life."

PUTTING PRAYER INTO PRACTICE

To reach out to others in love, it is necessary to set your fears aside. When you act out of fear, you destroy the quality of life—both yours and that of those around you. Catch yourself today when you fail to reach out because of fear. Become aware of how fear robs you of the joy of loving.

PRAYER

Brother Jesus,
you acted with integrity and loved without fear.
Help me to put the *shoulds* and *musts* aside,
to let go of the burden of straightening others out,
to let go of my own shame and fear
so that I can accept myself as I am

and accept others as they are.
Only then can I live in the power of your love
and know the way, the truth and the life.

CANTICLE Canticle of St. Patrick

Evening Prayer

Begin with page 237.

SCRIPTURE *See page 250.*

REFLECTION

What fears did I identify in myself today? Was I gentle
with myself as I discovered my fears?

PRAYER

In the face of fear, Christ,
help me to remember that I have two choices:
your strength or my own weakness.

CANTICLE Canticle of Mary

Opening Song for Morning Prayer

SALUTATION

With dawn comes hope
and the promise of new possibilities.

SONG Isaiah 52:7-8

How beautiful upon the mountains
    are the feet of him who brings glad tidings,
Announcing peace, bearing good news,
    announcing salvation, and saying to Zion,
    "Your God is King!"

Hark! Your watchmen raise a cry,
    together they shout for joy,
For they see directly, before their eyes
    the LORD restoring Zion.

*Turn to the page with today's date for the continuation of
Morning Prayer.*

Opening Song for Evening Prayer

SALUTATION

In the beauty of the sunset
and the magnificence of the night sky,
I see your handiwork, O Lord.

SONG Psalm 9:1-3, 10-11, 19

I will give thanks to you, O LORD, with all my heart;
    I will declare all your wondrous deeds.
I will be glad and exult in you;
    I will sing praise to your name, Most High....

The LORD is a stronghold for the oppressed,
    a stronghold in times of distress.
They trust in you who cherish your name,
    for you forsake not those who seek you, O LORD....

For the needy shall not always be forgotten,
    nor shall the hope of the afflicted forever perish.

Turn to the page with today's date for the continuation of Evening Prayer.

Morning Prayer

Begin with page 252.

SCRIPTURE Luke 11:9-10

And I tell you, ask and you will receive; seek and you will find; knock and the door will be opened to you. For everyone who asks, receives; and the one who seeks, finds; and to the one who knocks, the door will be opened.

PUTTING PRAYER INTO PRACTICE

This Scripture passage is particularly applicable to self-knowledge and spiritual growth. Watch for the times today when you become disturbed over what someone says to you. Ask God for the wisdom to discover the roots of your disturbance. In this way you will gain insights into those areas in your life where improvement and healing are needed.

PRAYER

Giver of all things, help me to understand
that the more at ease I am with the truth in myself,
the more at ease I am with the truth in others.
I knock at the door of self-knowledge to seek release
from shame
and to ask for the ability to love myself as I am,
so that I can pass through the threshold to inner peace.

CANTICLE Wisdom Canticle

Evening Prayer

Begin with page 253.

SCRIPTURE *See page 254.*

REFLECTION

What am I doing to be at ease with the truth about myself?

PRAYER

When I am at peace, Lord,
nothing anyone does or says
can disturb me.
Thanks for the gift of your peace,
and the grace not to settle for anything less.

CANTICLE Canticle of Zechariah

Morning Prayer

Begin with page 252.

SCRIPTURE Luke 12:16-21

Then [Jesus] told them a parable. "There was a rich man whose land produced a bountiful harvest. He asked himself, 'What shall I do, for I do not have space to store my harvest?' And he said, 'This is what I shall do: I shall tear down my barns and build larger ones. There I shall store all my grain and other goods and I shall say to myself, "Now as for you, you have so many good things stored up for many years, rest, eat, drink, be merry!" But God said to him, 'You fool, this night your life will be demanded of you; and the things you have prepared, to whom will they belong?' Thus will it be for the one who stores up treasure for himself but is not rich in what matters to God."

PUTTING PRAYER INTO PRACTICE

Today is World Food Day. Share your treasure with someone who is in need of food or medical care.

PRAYER

Creation groans,
children wail,
men shudder,
women turn in shame
when little ones die
and no one asks why.

CANTICLE Canticle of St. Patrick

Evening Prayer

Begin with page 253.

SCRIPTURE *See page 256.*

REFLECTION

Why, do you think, in a world where the grain supply alone is enough to meet everyone's nutritional needs one and one-half times over, forty thousand children die each day from malnutrition?

PRAYER

Let me dance through the fields and share the harvest, for I celebrate my oneness with all of creation.

CANTICLE Canticle of St. Francis

Morning Prayer

Begin with page 252.

SCRIPTURE Luke 12:22b-24

Therefore, I tell you, do not worry about your life and what you eat, or about your body and what you will wear. For life is more than food and the body more than clothing. Notice the ravens: they do not sow or reap; they have neither storehouse nor barn, yet God feeds them. How much more important are you than birds!

PUTTING PRAYER INTO PRACTICE

In this age of mounting medical costs and increased life span, it is normal for people to worry about providing for their old age. "We don't want to be a burden to our children or society," they say. But this train of thought leads people to care only for themselves. Even the elderly who are financially fit often live lonely, alienated lives. What is life about if it is not about caring for one another? While a certain amount of savings is appropriate, the person who spends his or her life caring for others, rather than laying up treasure, is the person who lives life at its deepest, fullest level. Reach out today to a stranger or contact an old friend. If you are homebound, do it by phone.

PRAYER

> You, God, are my security.
> On you alone I depend.
> All else is temporary,
> an illusion which vanishes
> in the light of eternity.

CANTICLE Canticle of Mary

Evening Prayer

Begin with page 253.

SCRIPTURE *See page 258.*

REFLECTION

> Why is it so hard for me to give my cares about old age,
> sickness and loneliness to God?

PRAYER

> Spirit of Life,
> You captivate with your charm!
> You care for the souls
> caught up in obedience
> to the divine.

CANTICLE Canticle of Judith

Morning Prayer

Begin with page 252.

SCRIPTURE Luke 11:42-46

"Woe to you Pharisees! You pay tithes of mint and of rue and of every garden herb, but you pay no attention to judgment and to love for God. These you should have done, without overlooking the others. Woe to you Pharisees! You love the seat of honor in synagogues and greetings in marketplaces. Woe to you! You are like unseen graves over which people unknowingly walk."

Then one of the scholars of the law said to him in reply, "Teacher, by saying this you are insulting us too." And he said, "Woe also to you scholars of the law! You impose on people burdens hard to carry, but you yourselves do not lift one finger to touch them."

PUTTING PRAYER INTO PRACTICE

Legalities, insurance and property values often keep us from living gospel values. Watch for the times today when you hesitate to help someone because of the letter of the law.

PRAYER

Deliver me, Father, from making choices
based on status, economics or legal liability.
These are false gods which lead to false security.
Instead, may I dare to risk some money or some time
to ease another's burdens.

Lead me, Lord, to live in the spirit of the law
rather than the letter of the law.

CANTICLE Canticle of St. Patrick

Evening Prayer

Begin with page 253.

SCRIPTURE *See page 260.*

REFLECTION

Refresh yourself today in the gospel message, which
calls us to a life of simplicity. How can you respond?

PRAYER

Thank you, Brother Jesus, for easing my burdens
and cutting through the clutter of complications.
My soul rests in you.

CANTICLE Canticle of Zechariah

Morning Prayer

Begin with page 252.

SCRIPTURE Psalm 51:12

A clean heart create for me, O God,
and a steadfast spirit renew within me.

COMMENTARY

Novenas and prayer cards sometimes lead people astray
with their never-fail promises. If prayer were that easy,
we'd all be rich, happy, in good health and at peace! No,
prayer is hard work, for it involves a cleansing process.
In a sense, prayer is forgiveness. The more one stands
before God in nakedness, humble and aware of the need
for forgiveness, the more one grows in intimacy with the
Creator. Equally difficult is the act of forgiving. When we
are without resentment or mistrust for those people who
have hurt us, we are living in a state of prayer or
communion with the divine.

PRAYER

It is the forgiving heart,
free of resentment and retribution,
that hears your voice, O Lord.
In silence, now, I seek your mercy
and, in turn, grant my forgiveness
to anyone who has brought pain or injury to me
or to someone I love.

CANTICLE Canticle of Judith

Evening Prayer

Begin with page 253.

SCRIPTURE *See page 262.*

REFLECTION

Pray again the prayer above. Then sit for a long period in silence, allowing the Spirit to enter and cleanse you.

PRAYER

Lord, I let go
of my anger and hurt
and I forgive *[mention name or names]*
for their offense against *[yourself or a loved one]*.

CANTICLE Canticle of Zechariah

Morning Prayer

Begin with page 252.

SCRIPTURE Luke 12:2-3

There is nothing concealed that will not be revealed, nor secret that will not be known. Therefore, whatever you have said in the darkness will be heard in the light, and what you have whispered behind closed doors will be proclaimed on the housetops.

PUTTING PRAYER INTO PRACTICE

Alcoholics Anonymous teaches that we are as sick as our secrets. What secrets do you have to bring to the light? What are you ashamed of? Expose these "rascals" to the light and to God, but don't dwell on your shame. You are a human being with weaknesses. Acknowledge the need for God's grace to overcome these weaknesses and move on from there.

PRAYER

For the courage, strength and grace
to expose my "shadows" to the light,
I pray to you, merciful Master.

CANTICLE Canticle of Mary

Evening Prayer

Begin with page 253.

SCRIPTURE *See page 264.*

REFLECTION

What do I say behind people's backs that I would not say to their faces? How do I feel about myself when I participate in gossip?

PRAYER

Let my speech be the product of a pure heart
or let me remain silent.

CANTICLE Wisdom Canticle

Morning Prayer

Begin with page 252.

SCRIPTURE Matthew 4:4b

One does not live by bread alone, but by every word that comes forth from the mouth of God.

COMMENTARY

Monsignor Hildebrand, a Chicago priest active in the civil rights movement, always said, "The poor do not need only bread—they need beauty too." The beauty he referred to was individual creativity. This may take the form of poetry, song, picture, dance or a project. As long as it is an expression coming out of inner beauty, it is unique and authentic.

PRAYER

Located within is a yearning to create.
Guide me, God, in giving bloom to my interior garden.

CANTICLE Wisdom Canticle

Evening Prayer

Begin with page 253.

SCRIPTURE *See page 266.*

REFLECTION

Did I unlock any of my creative potential today? Did I
help anybody else unlock creative potential?

PRAYER

Maker of Magic, wise Wizard and Starkeeper,
I marvel at your merriment,
for from you comes the unfathomable urge
to explode into spontaneous expression
of word, song and dance.

CANTICLE Canticle of Judith

Opening Song for Morning Prayer

SALUTATION

O Holy Spirit, inspire me
with divine potential this day!

SONG Psalm 1:1-3

Happy the man who follows not
    the counsel of the wicked
Nor walks in the way of sinners,
    nor sits in the company of the insolent,
But delights in the law of the LORD
    and meditates on his law day and night.
He is like a tree
    planted near running water,
That yields its fruit in due season,
    and whose leaves never fade.
    [Whatever he does, prospers.]

*Turn to the page with today's date for the continuation of
Morning Prayer.*

Opening Song for Evening Prayer

SALUTATION

To you, Yahweh, I give
the burdens and cares of the day.
Restore my soul and renew my spirit
as I slumber.

SONG Psalm 33:1-4; 21-22

Exult, you just, in the LORD;
    praise from the upright is fitting.
Give thanks to the LORD on the harp,
    with the ten-stringed lute chant his praises.
Sing to him a new song;
    pluck the strings skillfully, with shouts of gladness.
For upright is the word of the LORD,
    and all his works are trustworthy....

For in him our hearts rejoice;
    in his holy name we trust.
May your kindness, O LORD, be upon us
    who have put our hope in you.

Turn to the page with today's date for the continuation of Evening Prayer.

Morning Prayer

Begin with page 268.

SCRIPTURE Ezekiel 45:1-3

When you apportion the land into inheritances, you shall put apart a sacred tract of land for the LORD, twenty-five thousand cubits long and twenty thousand wide; its whole area shall be sacred. Of this land a square plot, five hundred by five hundred cubits, surrounded by a space of fifty cubits, shall be assigned to the sanctuary. Also from this sector measure off a strip, twenty-five thousand cubits long and ten thousand wide, within which shall be the sanctuary, the holy of holies.

PUTTING PRAYER INTO PRACTICE

If you are not already tithing, try it. Not only will it unleash God's generosity with you, but also God's generosity to you, through divine providence. Give especially to a charity or a needy person in your own town. Could hunger and poverty be eliminated if everyone tithed?

PRAYER

To live a life of prayer is to realize
that I own nothing.
All comes to me through you, God,
and goes out from me in your name.

CANTICLE Canticle of St. Francis

Evening Prayer

Begin with page 269.

SCRIPTURE *See page 270.*

REFLECTION

Am I afraid to tithe? If so, I'll start slowly and do it only a month at a time, now and then.

PRAYER

Even in my need, Lord,
I will try to give one tenth,
trusting in you
for my daily bread.

CANTICLE Canticle of Mary

Morning Prayer

Begin with page 268.

SCRIPTURE Ephesians 5:17-20

Therefore, do not continue in ignorance, but try to understand what is the will of the Lord. ...[B]e filled with the Spirit, addressing one another [in] psalms and hymns and spiritual songs, singing and playing to the Lord in your hearts, giving thanks always and for everything in the name of our Lord Jesus Christ to God the Father....

WORDS OF WISDOM

Let us always desire the happy life from the Lord God and always pray for it. But for this very reason we turn our mind to the task of prayer at appointed hours, since that desire grows lukewarm, so to speak, from our involvement in other concerns and occupations. We remind ourselves through the words of prayer to focus our attention on the object of our desire; otherwise, the desire that began to grow lukewarm may grow chill altogether and may be totally extinguished unless it is repeatedly stirred into flame.

Therefore, when the Apostle says, "Let your petitions become known before God," this should not be taken in the sense that they are in fact becoming known to God who certainly knew them even before they were made, but that they are becoming known to us before God through submission and not before men through boasting. (St. Augustine)[5]

PRAYER

> Give me, O Lord, the grace
> to work for the things I ask for. (St. Thomas More)

CANTICLE Wisdom Canticle

Evening Prayer

Begin with page 269.

SCRIPTURE *See page 272.*

REFLECTION

> When I spend less time in prayer, do I get more caught
> up with worldly things? Does the discipline of regular
> prayer improve my state of serenity?

PRAYER

> Anytime, anywhere,
> I can, by my prayer,
> be connected to you,
> divine Source of wisdom and love.
> You are my stronghold;
> to you I give thanks
> and lift my voice in praise!

CANTICLE Canticle of Judith

Morning Prayer

Begin with page 268.

SCRIPTURE Isaiah 55:8-9, 11

> For my thoughts are not your thoughts,
>   nor are your ways my ways, says the LORD.
> As high as the heavens are above the earth,
>   so high are my ways above your ways
>   and my thoughts above your thoughts....
>
> So shall my word be
>   that goes forth from my mouth;
> It shall not return to me void,
>   but shall do my will,
>   achieving the end for which I sent it.

PUTTING PRAYER INTO PRACTICE

If you are too attached to the outcome of a situation you tend to force results without realizing it. Notice how hard you work to get your way rather than just allowing things to fall into place. Besides using up energy, you create much stress and tension when you struggle for a particular outcome. Take your eye off the end result and focus on the process. Act and think according to your highest light and then trust that matters will unfold exactly as they should.

PRAYER

Teach me humility, Lord—
to know that *my* answer is not always *the* answer,
and teach me restraint
so that I will not force my expectations on others.

CANTICLE Canticle of Mary

Evening Prayer

Begin with page 269.

SCRIPTURE *See page 274.*

REFLECTION

Did I spend my energy shining today or did I waste it
trying to control or force things my way?

PRAYER

Thank you, Lord,
for revealing to me how everything—
even the events that appear to be tragedies—
works to serve your divine purpose.

CANTICLE Wisdom Canticle

Morning Prayer

Begin with page 268.

SCRIPTURE Luke 12:47-48

That servant who knew his master's will but did not make preparations nor act in accord with his will shall be beaten severely; and the servant who was ignorant of his master's will but acted in a way deserving of a severe beating shall be beaten only lightly. Much will be required of the person entrusted with much, and still more will be demanded of the person entrusted with more.

PUTTING PRAYER INTO PRACTICE

By your commitment to daily prayer, you are striving to understand God's will. In every situation you meet today, work to build bridges of peace and understanding. Do not give in to gossip. Remember, the more wisdom God gives you, the more God expects from you in the line of service.

PRAYER

Protect me, Lord, from self-righteousness.
Let me not be exalted by my gifts or spiritual knowledge!
All that I am I offer to you.

CANTICLE Canticle of St. Patrick

Evening Prayer

Begin with page 269.

SCRIPTURE *See page 276.*

REFLECTION

Do I feel smug in my knowledge of God and his
teachings? Do I feel superior and use my wisdom to
judge and criticize others?

PRAYER

Christ, with your light,
we can turn our churches
into sacred centers of healing and forgiveness
and drive out the false pride
which causes elitism and segregation.

CANTICLE Canticle of Mary

Morning Prayer

Begin with page 268.

SCRIPTURE Ephesians 3:14b-19

...I kneel before the Father, from whom every family in heaven and on earth is named, that he may grant you in accord with the riches of his glory to be strengthened with power through his Spirit in the inner self, and that Christ may dwell in your hearts through faith; that you, rooted and grounded in love, may have strength to comprehend with all the holy ones what is the breadth and length and height and depth, and to know the love of Christ that surpasses knowledge, so that you may be filled with all the fullness of God.

PUTTING PRAYER INTO PRACTICE

Today is full of surprises and each surprise has the potential to provide you with a special gift or lesson.

PRAYER

With delight, Lord, I await
the surprises that today will bring.
Help me to discover the message
that comes with each moment.

CANTICLE Canticle of St. Patrick

Evening Prayer

Begin with page 269.

SCRIPTURE *See page 278.*

REFLECTION

How did I benefit from my surprises today?

PRAYER

In thanksgiving for your providence
and the lessons it teaches,
I pray to you, all-knowing God.

CANTICLE Wisdom Canticle

Morning Prayer

Begin with page 268.

SCRIPTURE Jeremiah 18:6b

Indeed, like clay in the hand of the potter, so are you in my hand....

COMMENTARY

According to an Irish legend, St. Peter refused to admit Jack, a miserly Irishman, into heaven because he was so stingy with his money. The devil also refused to accept him because he wasn't bad enough. With nowhere to go, it became Jack's destiny to roam the world with a lantern—hence the term *jack-o-lantern*.

At harvest time, usually around Halloween, we make jack-o-lanterns out of pumpkins. But a preacher suggested another analogy for jack-o-lanterns: pumpkins that allow themselves to be molded by their maker so that light can shine out from them. Not all pumpkins in the pumpkin patch are willing to empty themselves, so most remain heavy and puffed up with self. What kind of pumpkin are you?

PRAYER

May I ripen in trust
and grow golden in wisdom
so that I willingly fall into your hands,
divine Harvester.
Eagerly I seek

your emptying embrace
and await your enlightenment.

CANTICLE Canticle of Mary

Evening Prayer

Begin with page 269.

SCRIPTURE *See page 280.*

REFLECTION

Am I willing to become a jack-o-lantern or am I content to
vegetate in the pumpkin patch?

PRAYER

Lord of Love,
you invite me constantly into your arms.
I tremble at your touch,
which brings death to self
and light to spirit.

CANTICLE Wisdom Canticle

Morning Prayer

Begin with page 268.

SCRIPTURE Ephesians 4:1-6

I, then, a prisoner for the Lord, urge you to live in a manner worthy of the call you have received, with all humility and gentleness, with patience, bearing with one another through love, striving to preserve the unity of the spirit through the bond of peace: one body and one Spirit, as you were also called to the one hope of your call; one Lord, one faith, one baptism, one God and Father of all, who is over all and through all and in all.

WORDS OF WISDOM

Every day opens and closes like a flower, noiseless, effortless. Divine peace glows on all the majestic landscape like the silent, enthusiastic joy that sometimes transforms a noble face. (American naturalist John Muir)

PRAYER

May I, too, be transformed by joy
and radiate that nobleness of character
that comes from serenity of soul.

CANTICLE Canticle of Mary

Evening Prayer

Begin with page 269.

SCRIPTURE *See page 282.*

REFLECTION

Accept yourself fully as you are right now. Rest in the confidence that God accepts and loves you just as you are.

PRAYER

Keep me from despairing, Lord.
When I sink into selfishness,
your hand alone can pluck me
from the mire of self-pity
and wash me with a tide of self-esteem.
Come, Lord, rescue me from my apathy!

CANTICLE Canticle of Zechariah

Morning Prayer

Begin with page 268.

SCRIPTURE Luke 18:9-14

[Jesus] then addressed this parable to those who were convinced of their own righteousness and despised everyone else. "Two people went up to the temple area to pray; one was a Pharisee and the other was a tax collector. The Pharisee took up his position and spoke this prayer to himself, 'O God, I thank you that I am not like the rest of humanity—greedy, dishonest, adulterous— or even like this tax collector. I fast twice a week, and I pay tithes on my whole income.' But the tax collector stood off at a distance and would not even raise his eyes to heaven but beat his breast and prayed, 'O God, be merciful to me a sinner.' I tell you, the latter went home justified, not the former; for everyone who exalts himself will be humbled, and the one who humbles himself will be exalted."

PUTTING PRAYER INTO PRACTICE

Not words but action and attitude determine authentic discipleship. Does your attitude separate you from people you perceive as inferior or different? Take some kind of action today that will unite you with one person or a class of persons that you do not usually spend time with.

PRAYER

Diminish my fear of differences, Lord. Give me the grace
to reach out today to a prostitute, a prisoner, a Buddhist,
a poor person, a rich person or anyone that I perceive as
different from myself.

CANTICLE Canticle of St. Patrick

Evening Prayer

Begin with page 269.

SCRIPTURE *See page 284.*

REFLECTION

Do I live in a homogeneous world? Are most people
around me the same color, economic level and social
class as I am? Do we all love and hate the same things
and people? How does this attitude clash with
discipleship?

PRAYER

Divine Protector, shoulder my burdens now
as I prepare to rest.
In gratefulness and trust, Lord,
I lay down to sleep
and place my body and soul in your care.

CANTICLE Canticle of Judith

Morning Prayer

Begin with page 268.

SCRIPTURE Romans 8:18-25

I consider that the sufferings of this present time are as
nothing compared with the glory to be revealed for us.
For creation awaits with eager expectation the revelation
of the children of God; for creation was made subject to
futility, not of its own accord but because of the one who
subjected it, in hope that creation itself would be set free
from slavery to corruption and share in the glorious
freedom of the children of God. We know that all
creation is groaning in labor pains even until now; and
not only that, but we ourselves, who have the first fruits
of the Spirit, we also groan within ourselves as we wait
for adoption, the redemption of our bodies. For in hope
we were saved. Now hope that sees for itself is not hope.
For who hopes for what one sees? But if we hope for
what we do not see, we wait with endurance.

PUTTING PRAYER INTO PRACTICE

Notice today the times when you feel hopeful and the
times when you feel hopeless.

PRAYER

Divine Spirit, you groan within me,
even though I may not be conscious of it.
I need not call your name
for you are already there.
My task, then, is simply
to see you in all creation.

CANTICLE Canticle of Judith

Evening Prayer

Begin with page 269.

SCRIPTURE *See page 286.*

REFLECTION

Today did I discover how hope is working in my life? Did
I remember, when I felt hopeless, to see God in all
creation?

PRAYER

Glory and praise to you, Creator God,
in thanksgiving for the gift of hope.

CANTICLE Wisdom Canticle

Morning Prayer

Begin with page 268.

SCRIPTURE Ephesians 5:6-14a

Let no one deceive you with empty arguments, for because of these things the wrath of God is coming upon the disobedient. So do not be associated with them. For you were once darkness, but now you are light in the Lord. Live as children of light, for light produces every kind of goodness and righteousness and truth. Try to learn what is pleasing to the Lord. Take no part in the fruitless works of darkness; rather expose them, for it is shameful even to mention the things done by them in secret; but everything exposed by the light becomes visible, for everything that becomes visible is light.

PUTTING PRAYER INTO PRACTICE

Keep in mind that you are a child of the light. In situations you may face today where there is gloom and negativity, look for the light side. Communicate the positive aspects of the situation to those around you and encourage them to follow their own higher light.

PRAYER

Help me, Divine Spirit, to take myself lightly
so that you may be able to shine through me.

CANTICLE Canticle of Mary

Evening Prayer

Begin with page 269.

SCRIPTURE *See page 288.*

REFLECTION

What did I do today to counteract the works of darkness
or negative forces in my life?

PRAYER

On this night of hobgoblins and ghosts,
I reach out for your power and strength, Almighty God,
to transform the dark into day,
and overcome evil with good.

CANTICLE Canticle of St. Francis

Notes

[1] From *De Anima*.

[2] From *Aurora Leigh*, Book VII.

[3] From *St. Francis of Assisi: Omnibus of Sources,* edited by Marion A. Habig, copyright ©1973 by Franciscan Herald Press. Used with the permission of Franciscan Press.

[4] St. Bernard of Clairvaux, "Sermon on the Annunciation of the Blessed Virgin," French trsl. M.M. Dauy, Oeuvres de Saint Bernard, vol. i, p. 106.

[5] The excerpt from *The Liturgy of the Hours,* copyright ©1975, International Committee on English in the Liturgy, Inc. All rights reserved.

November

Opening Song for Morning Prayer

SALUTATION

> Rise up in splendor! Your light has come,
>> the glory of the Lord shines upon you. (Isaiah 60:1)

SONG Psalm 66:1-4

> Shout joyfully to God, all you on earth,
>> sing praise to the glory of his name;
>> proclaim his glorious praise.
> Say to God, "How tremendous are your deeds!
>> for your great strength your enemies fawn upon you.
> Let all on earth worship and sing praise to you,
>> sing praise to your name!"

Turn to the page with today's date for the continuation of Morning Prayer.

Opening Song for Evening Prayer

SALUTATION

Restore and replenish my spirit, Lord,
as night approaches.

SONG Psalm 66:5-9

Come and see the works of God,
    his tremendous deeds among men.
He has changed the sea into dry land;
    through the river they passed on foot;
    therefore let us rejoice in him.
He rules by his might forever;
    his eyes watch the nations;
    rebels may not exalt themselves.
Bless our God, you peoples,
    loudly sound his praise;
He has given life to our souls,
    and has not let our feet slip.

Turn to the page with today's date for the continuation of Evening Prayer.

Morning Prayer

Begin with page 292.

SCRIPTURE 1 John 3:1-3

See what love the Father has bestowed on us that we may be called the children of God. Yet so we are. The reason the world does not know us is that it did not know him. Beloved, we are God's children now; what we shall be has not yet been revealed. We do know that when it is revealed we shall be like him, for we shall see him as he is. Everyone who has this hope based on him makes himself pure, as he is pure.

MEDITATION PRAYER

In the beginning when we first started, God,
it was easy.
You carried me on your shoulders
and protected me with your strength.

After a while, you asked me
to stand on my own and walk alongside you.
The more our friendship grew,
the more I dared to take unknown paths.
At times you would disappear
and then return.
And with each absence,
I was strengthened.

I chuckle now as I plod along
turning controversial corners
and struggling to bring your peace

into the wildest thickets.

How different I thought things would be
when we first started.

CANTICLE Canticle of Judith

Evening Prayer

Begin with page 293.

SCRIPTURE *See page 294.*

REFLECTION

The challenge of sainthood is to go where love takes me.
Am I willing to go?

PRAYER

I smile, Father God,
for I am one of your children,
and you will not leave me orphaned.
With a grateful heart,
I give thanks.

CANTICLE Canticle of St. Francis

Morning Prayer

Begin with page 292.

SCRIPTURE Romans 6:1-9

What then shall we say? Shall we persist in sin that grace may abound? Of course not! How can we who died to sin yet live in it? Or are you unaware that we who were baptized into Christ Jesus were baptized into his death? We were indeed buried with him through baptism into his death, so that, just as Christ was raised from the dead by the glory of the Father, we too might live in newness of life.

For if we have grown into union with him through a death like his, we shall also be united with him in the resurrection. We know that our old self was crucified with him, so that our sinful body might be done away with, that we might no longer be in slavery to sin. For a dead person has been absolved from sin. If, then, we have died with Christ, we believe that we shall also live with him. We know that Christ, raised from the dead, dies no more; death no longer has power over him.

WORDS OF WISDOM

The flesh is the apparel of the soul, which is clothed with a body as a garment. (St. Ambrose)

PRAYER

We pray and celebrate
with those dearly departed souls
we knew and loved so well.
Happy are they who have learned the blessing
of going naked into eternity!

CANTICLE Canticle of St. Francis

Evening Prayer

Begin with page 293.

SCRIPTURE *See page 296.*

REFLECTION

Will I be ready when death calls? Can I let go of the
things of the flesh and dance happily into the arms of the
Creator?

PRAYER

Thank you for preparing a place for me, God.
I rest in confidence because you promise
I will be with you in eternity.

CANTICLE Canticle of Mary

Morning Prayer

Begin with page 292.

SCRIPTURE Matthew 25:31a, 32b-40

When the Son of Man comes in his glory...he will separate them one from another, as a shepherd separates the sheep from the goats. He will place the sheep on his right and the goats on his left. Then the king will say to those on his right, "Come, you who are blessed by my Father. Inherit the kingdom prepared for you from the foundation of the world. For I was hungry and you gave me food, I was thirsty and you gave me drink, a stranger and you welcomed me, naked and you clothed me, ill and you cared for me, in prison, and you visited me." Then the righteous will answer him and say, "Lord when did we see you hungry and feed you, or thirsty and give you drink? When did we see you a stranger and welcome you, or naked and clothe you? When did we see you ill or in prison, and visit you?" And the king will say to them in reply, "Amen, I say to you, whatever you did for one of these least brothers of mine, you did for me."

MEDITATION

In the above Gospel story, what did the Son of Man say to the goats on his left? Do you see God in other people, especially those people who nag, whine, criticize, blame others for their problems, talk about their illnesses? Do you help those who are ungrateful and cranky? Do you share precious moments with the ill? the homeless? the imprisoned? or someone in your own family who may be ostracized by the rest of the family because he or she is on drugs, gay, living in sin?

PRAYER

Lord, that I might see your face
in those that are hungry for attention and acceptance,
I pray to you.

CANTICLE Canticle of St. Patrick

Evening Prayer

Begin with page 293.

SCRIPTURE *See page 298.*

REFLECTION Am I a sheep or a goat?

PRAYER

What consolation it gives me,
King of the Universe,
to hear your concern
for the least in your kingdom.
You are indeed a merciful Creator,
building on the foundation
of justice and love.

CANTICLE Canticle of Judith

Morning Prayer

Begin with page 292.

SCRIPTURE Philippians 1:18c-24

Indeed, I shall continue to rejoice, for I know that this will result in deliverance for me through your prayers and support from the Spirit of Jesus Christ. My eager expectation and hope is that I shall not be put to shame in any way, but that with all boldness, now as always, Christ will be magnified in my body, whether by life or by death. For to me life is Christ, and death is gain. If I go on living in the flesh, that means fruitful labor for me. And I do not know which I shall choose. I am caught between the two. I long to depart this life and be with Christ, [for] that is far better. Yet that I remain [in] the flesh is more necessary for your benefit.

WORDS OF WISDOM

Jesus was not willing to compromise by accepting the Messiahship and resorting to violence nor was he willing to tailor his words to suit the authorities. The only alternative was to die. In these circumstances, death was the only way of continuing to serve mankind, the only way of speaking to the worldly (John 7:1-4), the only way of witnessing to the kingdom. Deeds speak louder than words but death speaks louder than deeds. Jesus died so that the kingdom might come. (Albert Nolan)[1]

PRAYER

> Let me reach the point,
> eternal Lord,
> where I can celebrate death
> and rejoice at the soul's union with you.

CANTICLE Canticle of St. Francis

Evening Prayer

Begin with page 293.

SCRIPTURE *See page 300.*

REFLECTION

> To what extent do I fear death, the loss of a loved one or
> being alone and uncared for in my old age? How much do
> these fears imprison and hinder me from serving God
> and others in love?

PRAYER

> As I choose to let go of fear,
> you are there, Lord,
> to fill the empty space.

CANTICLE Canticle of Mary

Morning Prayer

Begin with page 292.

SCRIPTURE Luke 19:1-10

[Jesus] came to Jericho and intended to pass through the town. Now a man there named Zacchaeus, who was a chief tax collector and also a wealthy man, was seeking to see who Jesus was; but he could not see him because of the crowd, for he was short in stature. So he ran ahead and climbed a sycamore tree in order to see Jesus, who was about to pass that way. When he reached the place, Jesus looked up and said to him, "Zacchaeus, come down quickly, for today I must stay at your house." And he came down quickly and received him with joy. When they all saw this, they began to grumble, saying, "He has gone to stay at the house of a sinner." But Zacchaeus stood there and said to the Lord, "Behold, half my possessions, Lord, I shall give to the poor, and if I have extorted anything from anyone I shall repay it four times over." And Jesus said to him, "Today salvation has come to this house because this man too is a descendant of Abraham. For the Son of Man has come to seek and to save what was lost."

WORDS OF WISDOM

Jesus loved all men and lived in solidarity with all mankind. And for this very reason, Jesus sided with the poor and the oppressed, with those who had nothing to recommend them except their humanity, with those who were excluded by others. Solidarity with the nobodies of this world, the discarded people, is the only concrete way of living out a solidarity with mankind. (Albert Nolan)[2]

PRAYER

Give me the humility, Lord,
to exclude no one from my friendship,
including those parts of me
that I would like to ignore.

CANTICLE Canticle of St. Patrick

Evening Prayer

Begin with page 293.

SCRIPTURE *See page 302.*

REFLECTION In what ways am I in solidarity with the poor?

PRAYER

Thank you for forgiving me when I fall, Lord.
Your mercy and compassion endure forever.

CANTICLE Canticle of St. Francis

Morning Prayer

Begin with page 292.

SCRIPTURE Matthew 21:12a

Jesus entered the temple area and drove out all those engaged in selling and buying there.

COMMENTARY

It is Meister Eckhart's contention that the soul resembles God more than any other creation. This is the temple that God wants empty so that he alone can possess it. Behold, however, how people bargain with God—doing a fast or a vigil in order to obtain a special favor. It is only when we rid ourselves of these ego connections that the beauty of our temple, our soul, will be pure and shine in splendor.

PRAYER

Drive out from my soul, creator God,
the merchant mentality,
so that it may reflect
the pure radiance of your being.

CANTICLE Wisdom Canticle

Evening Prayer

Begin with page 293.

SCRIPTURE Matthew 21:12a

Jesus entered the temple area and drove out all those engaged in selling and buying there.

REFLECTION

In what ways do I bargain with God, selfishly seeking gain here on earth or a ticket to eternity?

PRAYER

Thank you, gentle God,
for the beauty of my soul.
Help me to grow in appreciation
of this magnificent temple.
Alone, I will seek you
and find you
in this holy place.

CANTICLE Canticle of Zechariah

Morning Prayer

Begin with page 292.

SCRIPTURE Romans 12:4-8

For as in one body we have many parts, and all the parts do not have the same function, so we, though many, are one body in Christ and individually parts of one another. Since we have gifts that differ according to the grace given to us, let us exercise them: if prophecy, in proportion to the faith; if ministry, in ministering; if one is a teacher, in teaching; if one exhorts, in exhortation; if one contributes, in generosity; if one is over others, with diligence; if one does acts of mercy, with cheerfulness.

PUTTING PRAYER INTO PRACTICE

To use your gifts, you must first be convinced that you have them. You were created in the image and likeness of God and you have something special to do that no one else can accomplish. Today, identify your gifts if you don't know them already. If you need help, ask a friend or a coworker how he or she thinks you could use your abilities to make the world a better place.

PRAYER

As I see my abilities as gifts from you, creator God, rather than something I have developed on my own, I will feel freer
to acknowledge and share those gifts with others.

CANTICLE Canticle of Judith

Evening Prayer

Begin with page 293.

SCRIPTURE *See page 306.*

REFLECTION

When I look in the mirror, do I see the image and
likeness of God?

PRAYER

Thank you, divine Master,
for fashioning me in your image and likeness.
It is difficult, sometimes,
for me to see my magnificence
because I think, somehow, I created myself.

CANTICLE Canticle of Mary

Opening Song for Morning Prayer

SALUTATION

Arise, my sleeping soul.
Awaken to your destiny.
Devour my despair, Lord,
so that I may walk in joy!

SONG Psalm 138:1-3

I will give thanks to you, O LORD, with all my heart,
  [for you have heard the words of my mouth;]
    in the presence of the angels I will sing your praise;
I will worship at your holy temple
  and give thanks to your name,
Because of your kindness and your truth;
  for you have made great above all things
  your name and your promise.
When I called, you answered me;
  you built up strength within me.

Turn to the page with today's date for the continuation of Morning Prayer.

Opening Song for Evening Prayer

SALUTATION

As dark descends, I wait for you, Yahweh!

SONG Psalm 138:4-8

All the kings of the earth shall give thanks to you,
O LORD,
when they hear the words of your mouth;
And they will sing of the ways of the LORD;
"Great is the glory of the LORD."
The LORD is exalted, yet the lowly he sees,
and the proud he knows from afar.

Though I walk amid distress, your preserve me;
against the anger of my enemies you raise your hand;
your right hand saves me.
The LORD will complete what he has done for me;
your kindness, O LORD, endures forever;
forsake not the work of your hands.

*Turn to the page with today's date for the continuation of
Evening Prayer.*

Morning Prayer

Begin with page 308.

SCRIPTURE Luke 14:25-33

Great crowds were traveling with him, and he turned and addressed them, "If anyone comes to me without hating his father and mother, wife and children, brothers and sisters, and even his own life, he cannot be my disciple. Whoever does not carry his own cross and come after me cannot be my disciple. Which of you wishing to construct a tower does not first sit down and calculate the cost to see if there is enough for its completion? Otherwise, after laying the foundation and finding himself unable to finish the work the onlookers should laugh at him and say, 'This one began to build but did not have the resources to finish.' Or what king marching into battle would not first sit down and decide whether with ten thousand troops he can successfully oppose another king advancing upon him with twenty thousand troops? But if not, while he is still far away, he will send a delegation to ask for peace terms. In the same way, everyone of you who does not renounce all his possessions cannot be my disciple."

PUTTING PRAYER INTO PRACTICE

Although we have obligations to our families, Christ tells us that family, possessions, even our own lives must not get in the way of discipleship. A commonplace application might be making a tough decision about where to spend family resources. For example, a family could decide not to spend money for purely cosmetic orthodontia in order to send money to the Third World, where children die at the rate of two per minute for lack of food and medical supplies.

PRAYER

Brother Jesus,
give me the maturity to count the cost
before setting out on the road to discipleship.

CANTICLE Canticle of St. Patrick

Evening Prayer

Begin with page 309.

SCRIPTURE *See page 310.*

REFLECTION

For what am I working each day? Where do my money and energy go? Am I laboring for the Kingdom of God or for selfish gain?

PRAYER

You invite me to help build your Kingdom, gentle Ruler. Take my resources, my time, money and energy, and put them to your service.

CANTICLE Canticle of Zechariah

Morning Prayer

Begin with page 308.

SCRIPTURE Philippians 3:7-8

...[W]hatever gains I had, these I have come to consider
a loss because of Christ. More than that, I even consider
everything as a loss because of the supreme good of
knowing Christ Jesus my Lord. For his sake I have
accepted the loss of all things and I consider them so
much rubbish, that I may gain Christ....

WORDS OF WISDOM

Self-importance is our greatest enemy. Think about
it—what weakens us is feeling offended by the deeds and
misdeeds of our fellow men. Our self-importance
requires that we spend most of our lives offended by
someone.... The burden of self-importance is a terrible
encumbrance. (Carlos Castañeda)[3]

PRAYER

Help me to understand, wise God,
that the greater my self-esteem
the less my need for self-importance.
Relieve me of the need to make others honor me,
for dignity comes only from the divine
and is developed in a life of integrity and service.

CANTICLE Canticle of Mary

Evening Prayer

Begin with page 309.

SCRIPTURE *See page 312.*

REFLECTION

At what times today did my pride or self-importance get in the way?

PRAYER

For the light to see
and the humor to laugh
at my own false pride,
I am grateful, Lord.

CANTICLE Wisdom Canticle

Morning Prayer

Begin with page 308.

SCRIPTURE Philippians 4:4-8

Rejoice in the Lord always. I shall say it again: rejoice!
Your kindness should be known to all. The Lord is near.
Have no anxiety at all, but in everything, by prayer and
petition, with thanksgiving, make your requests known
to God. Then the peace of God that surpasses all
understanding will guard your hearts and minds in
Christ Jesus.

Finally, brothers, whatever is true, whatever is
honorable, whatever is just, whatever is pure, whatever
is lovely, whatever is gracious, if there is any excellence
and if there is anything worthy of praise, think about
these things.

PUTTING PRAYER INTO PRACTICE

When you begin to worry today or feel anxious, shift
your thoughts to whatever is lovely and rejoice. If you
become upset over the world news or local gossip, say a
prayer of healing for the brokenness you perceive and
then shift your thoughts to the excellence and beauty
that is also in the world.

PRAYER

> Today, Lord, I will take a break
> from solving world problems.
> Instead, I will see and appreciate
> the goodness that surrounds me.

CANTICLE Canticle of St. Francis

Evening Prayer

Begin with page 309.

SCRIPTURE *See page 314.*

REFLECTION

Was I able to maintain a calm inner core of peace today?

Enter your reflections in your spiritual journal, if you are keeping one. If you answered yes to the above question, write the details of each experience in which you were able to turn away from anxiety and worry.

PRAYER

> For the faith to trust
> that all things will work for the good,
> I am grateful, loving and gracious God.

CANTICLE Canticle of Judith

Morning Prayer

Begin with page 308.

SCRIPTURE Luke 16:10-13

The person who is trustworthy in very small matters is also trustworthy in great ones; and the person who is dishonest in very small matters is also dishonest in great ones. If, therefore, you are not trustworthy with dishonest wealth, who will trust you with true wealth? If you are not trustworthy with what belongs to another, who will give you what is yours? No servant can serve two masters. He will either hate one and love the other, or be devoted to one and despise the other. You cannot serve God and mammon.

PUTTING PRAYER INTO PRACTICE

In yourself, watch for those small things in which you are not entirely ethical or honest. Beware, however, of watching for these things in others. Keep your eye on your own transgressions.

PRAYER

It is difficult, Lord,
to be honest about my shortcomings,
especially the little things
that constantly betray me.
Send me the stamina to persevere
through my small, daily transgressions.

CANTICLE Canticle of Zechariah

Evening Prayer

Begin with page 309.

SCRIPTURE *See page 316.*

REFLECTION

Was I able to look at some of my dark side and not turn
away or distract myself by finding fault with another?

PRAYER

I rejoice in your goodness, God,
for your mercy allows me
to accept that part of myself
which I hide from others.

CANTICLE Wisdom Canticle

Morning Prayer

Begin with page 308.

SCRIPTURE Mark 12:41-44

[Jesus] sat down opposite the treasury, and observed how the crowd put money into the treasury. Many rich people put in large sums. A poor widow also came and put in two small coins worth a few cents. Calling his disciples to himself, he said to them, "Amen, I say to you, this poor widow put in more than all the other contributors to the treasury. For they have all contributed from their surplus wealth, but she, from her poverty, has contributed all she had, her whole livelihood."

PUTTING PRAYER INTO PRACTICE

Are you holding out on God? Do you tithe? If you say you cannot afford to tithe, think of the Scripture reading. Make an accounting to the Lord today and decide what your fair share of return should be.

PRAYER

How shall I make a return to the LORD
for all the good he has done for me? (Psalm 116:12)

CANTICLE Canticle of St. Francis

Evening Prayer

Begin with page 309.

SCRIPTURE *See page 318.*

REFLECTION

Did I determine a fair share to return to the Lord and resolve to carry my decision out?

PRAYER

You bless me so bountifully, Lord,
yet I always get caught up in my need.
Forgive my lack of gratitude.

CANTICLE Canticle of Mary

Morning Prayer

Begin with page 308.

SCRIPTURE Luke 17:1-4

[J]esus said to his disciples, "Things that cause sin will inevitably occur, but woe to the person through whom they occur. It would be better for him if a millstone were put around his neck and he be thrown into the sea than for him to cause one of these little ones to sin. Be on your guard! If your brother sins, rebuke him; and if he repents, forgive him. And if he wrongs you seven times in one day and returns to you seven times saying, 'I am sorry,' you should forgive him."

PUTTING PRAYER INTO PRACTICE

How do you forgive? Do you say you forgive but in your heart remember the offense and let resentment build up? Today, let go of any resentment you may be harboring. If this seems impossible, get down on your knees and ask God's help in lifting this burden from you.

PRAYER

Teach me, Lord,
not only to forgive
but also to let go of hurt
so I can reach out
and love again.

CANTICLE Canticle of St. Patrick

Evening Prayer

Begin with page 309.

SCRIPTURE *See page 320.*

REFLECTION

Against whom am I harboring resentment? Was I able to let go of my anger today?

PRAYER

For all the times you have forgiven
and loved me in spite of my unworthiness,
I thank you, merciful God.

CANTICLE Canticle of Zechariah

Morning Prayer

Begin with page 308.

SCRIPTURE Romans 8:31-34a

What then shall we say to this? If God is for us, who can be against us? He who did not spare his own Son but handed him over for us all, how will he not also give us everything else along with him? Who will bring a charge against God's chosen ones? It is God who acquits us. Who will condemn?

PUTTING PRAYER INTO PRACTICE

Do not fear failure. Embrace it! Try something today that you always wanted to do but didn't for fear that you would not succeed. Try it now!

PRAYER

Give me the daring, Lord, to do the impossible
and the realization that, even if I fail,
I am still ahead for having tried.

CANTICLE Canticle of Mary

Evening Prayer

Begin with page 309.

SCRIPTURE *See page 322.*

REFLECTION

Did I laugh at failure today?

PRAYER

It feels so good, God,
to stretch and to grow
under your loving gaze.

CANTICLE Wisdom Canticle

Opening Song for Morning Prayer

SALUTATION

Awake, awake, put on strength,
...I, it is I who comfort you. (Isaiah 51:9a, 12a)

SONG Psalm 65:2-6

To you we owe our hymn of praise,
   O God, in Zion;
To you must vows be fulfilled,
   you who hear prayers.
To you all flesh must come
   because of wicked deeds.
We are overcome by our sins;
   it is you who pardon them.
Happy is the man you choose,
   and bring to dwell in your courts.
May we be filled with the good things of your house,
   the holy things of your temple!

With awe-inspiring deeds of justice you answer us,
   O God our Savior,
The hope of all the ends of the earth
   and of the distant seas.

Turn to the page with today's date for the continuation of Morning Prayer.

Opening Song for Evening Prayer

SALUTATION

I sing to you in thanksgiving and praise
as the day comes to a close,
caring and compassionate God.

SONG Psalm 65:10-14

You have visited the land and watered it;
    greatly you have enriched it.
God's watercourses are filled;
    you have prepared the grain.
Thus have you prepared the land:
    drenching its furrows,
    breaking up its clods,
Softening it with showers,
    blessing its yield.
You have crowned the year with your bounty,
    and your paths overflow with a rich harvest;
The untilled meadows overflow with it,
    and rejoicing clothes the hills.
The fields are garmented with flocks
    and the valleys blanketed with grain.
They shout and sing for joy.

Turn to the page with today's date for the continuation of Evening Prayer.

Morning Prayer

Begin with page 324.

SCRIPTURE Wisdom 7:24-28

For Wisdom is mobile beyond all motion,
    and she penetrates and pervades all things by reason
      of her purity.
For she is an aura of the might of God
    and a pure effusion of the glory of the Almighty;
    therefore nought that is sullied enters into her.
For she is the refulgence of eternal light,
    the spotless mirror of the power of God,
    the image of his goodness.
And she, who is one, can do all things,
    and renews everything while herself perduring;
And passing into holy souls from age to age
    she produces friends of God and prophets.
For there is nought God loves, be it not one who dwells
    with Wisdom.

PUTTING PRAYER INTO PRACTICE

Before you speak or act today, take a deep breath and
picture yourself as the wisest person on earth, a mirror
of divine light. With that thought in mind, proceed to
speak and act.

PRAYER

Help me to dwell in your wisdom,
almighty God.

CANTICLE Canticle of St. Patrick

Evening Prayer

Begin with page 325.

SCRIPTURE Wisdom 7:28

> For there is nought God loves, be it not one who dwells
> with wisdom.

REFLECTION

> At what times today did I speak and act wisely? How can
> I develop this ability?

Enter today's moments of wisdom in your journal, if you are
keeping one. Describe the thoughts and feelings that
surrounded these moments.

PRAYER

> Spirit of Wisdom,
> come find a home in my heart.

CANTICLE Wisdom Canticle

Morning Prayer

Begin with page 324.

SCRIPTURE Luke 17:7-10

Who among you would say to your servant who has just
come in from plowing or tending sheep in the field,
"Come here immediately and take your place at table?"
Would he not rather say to him, "Prepare something for
me to eat. Put on your apron and wait on me while I eat
and drink. You may eat and drink when I am finished"? Is
he grateful to that servant because he did what was
commanded? So should it be with you. When you have
done all you have been commanded, say, "We are
unprofitable servants; we have done what we were
obliged to do."

WORDS OF WISDOM

All that the beginner in prayer has to do—and you must
not forget this for it is important—is to labour and be
resolute and prepare yourself with all possible diligence
to bring your will into conformity with the will of God.
(Teresa of Avila)[4]

PRAYER

I am your humble servant, Lord,
striving to discern your will.

CANTICLE Canticle of Mary

Evening Prayer

Begin with page 325.

SCRIPTURE *See page 328.*

REFLECTION

Think about some of the things you have to do
tomorrow. Pick two or three and strive to discern how
the Lord would like you to handle them. Picture yourself
handling these situations as the Lord has directed you.

PRAYER

Oh, how joy consumes me
when I conform to your commandments,
Creator God!

CANTICLE Canticle of St. Francis

Morning Prayer

Begin with page 324.

SCRIPTURE Wisdom 15:10-12

Ashes his heart is! more worthless than earth is his
hope,
and more ignoble than clay his life;
Because he knew not the one who fashioned him,
and breathed into him a quickening soul,
and infused a vital spirit.
Instead, he esteemed our life a plaything,
and our span of life a holiday for gain;
"For one must," says he, "make profit every way, be it
even out of evil."

PUTTING PRAYER INTO PRACTICE

St. Elizabeth of Hungary knew her Maker and lived a life
that inspired others. She lived in the thirteenth century
and was married to King Louis, who did not approve of
his wife's charitable efforts—he thought them
undignified. One day, when St. Elizabeth was going with
an apron full of bread to feed the poor, she met her
husband on the road. Irritated, he asked her to open her
apron and when she did, so the legend goes, the bread
turned into roses. Later, Louis died at an early age, and
she was driven from the castle by her in-laws, who
ridiculed her. Instead of pitying herself, she contributed
the little she had to feed and care for the poor. Elizabeth
is the opposite of the man in today's Scripture reading.

PRAYER

> Without your divine inspiration,
> compassionate Creator,
> all work is drudgery.
> Infuse me with a vital spirit!

CANTICLE Canticle of St. Patrick

Evening Prayer

Begin with page 325.

SCRIPTURE *See page 330.*

REFLECTION

> Do I work with vision and joy in my heart, conscious of
> my Creator and my own ability to create?

PRAYER

> Your words, wise Master,
> keep me from a worthless life!

CANTICLE Wisdom Canticle

Morning Prayer

Begin with page 324.

SCRIPTURE Luke 17:20-22

Asked by the Pharisees when the kingdom of God would come, [Jesus] said in reply, "The coming of the kingdom of God cannot be observed, and no one will announce, 'Look, here it is,' or, 'There it is.' For behold, the kingdom of God is among you."

STORY

Once upon a time there was a man who left his quarrelsome family to find the Kingdom of God. He walked all day. At dark, he stopped in the woods to sleep. Before closing his eyes, he took off his shoes and pointed them in the direction he was traveling. During the night, a forest elf came and turned his shoes in the opposite direction. When the man awoke, he put his shoes on and continued walking. After a few hours, he noticed things that looked familiar. The further he walked, the more he recognized. Finally, he came to a house that looked like his home. He went into the house, greeted the occupants with love and lived happily ever after with his family—amid the Kingdom of God. (Author unknown)

PRAYER

Grant me the grace, God,
to build your kingdom
wherever I am.

CANTICLE Canticle of St. Patrick

Evening Prayer

Begin with page 325.

SCRIPTURE *See page 332.*

REFLECTION

Do I see God in the people and situations that surround me? Do I attempt to bring God's peace into the daily events of my life?

PRAYER

In love you fashioned me,
In love you transform me.
In love I give thanks!

CANTICLE Canticle of Mary

Morning Prayer

Begin with page 324.

SCRIPTURE Luke 21:19

By your patience you will secure your lives.

PUTTING PRAYER INTO PRACTICE

As the Church approaches the end of Ordinary Time and looks forward to Advent—a time of celebration, it is important to reflect on the meaning of Ordinary Time. Every life has its highs and lows, its times of sorrow and times of ecstasy. But most of life is ordinary. It is in making the most of ordinary times that you will need "the patience to secure your life."

Today, use every chance to express kindness and patience. When no one else is around, be kind to and patient with yourself.

PRAYER

Help me to develop a deep spirituality, Lord.
Give me a faith so firmly rooted
that I can transform the ordinary into the extraordinary
by the simple practice of patience.

CANTICLE Canticle of St. Francis

Evening Prayer

Begin with page 325.

SCRIPTURE *See page 334.*

REFLECTION

How can I develop this hidden power of patience?

PRAYER

I was amazed today, loving Parent,
by what happened when I took an extra few minutes
to be kind to and patient with those who passed my way.
For the self-composure that makes this possible,
I am truly grateful!

CANTICLE Wisdom Canticle

Morning Prayer

Begin with page 324.

SCRIPTURE Luke 18:35-43

Now as [Jesus] approached Jericho a blind man was sitting by the roadside begging, and hearing a crowd going by, he inquired what was happening. They told him "Jesus of Nazareth is passing by." He shouted, "Jesus, Son of David, have pity on me!" The people walking in front rebuked him, telling him to be silent, but he kept calling out all the more, "Son of David, have pity on me!" Then Jesus stopped and ordered that he be brought to him; and when he came near, Jesus asked him, "What do you want me to do for you?" He replied, "Lord, please let me see." Jesus told him, "Have sight, your faith has saved you." He immediately received his sight and followed him, giving glory to God. When they saw this, all the people gave praise to God.

MEDITATION EXERCISE

Sit quietly for a few moments. Breathing slowly, say either the Jesus Prayer or the Hail Mary for a minute or two. Ask Jesus to banish all negative thoughts and ego influences. When you are quiet and at peace, answer the question Jesus asked the blind man in today's Scripture reading: "What do you want me to do for you?" (Luke 18:41a).

Let your request break from your heart—let it be something deep and meaningful rather than a "quick fix" request such as weight loss or job promotion.

PRAYER

> I pray, Brother Jesus, for the initiative
> to grasp every opportunity
> to make my request become reality.

CANTICLE Canticle of Mary

Evening Prayer

Begin with page 325.

SCRIPTURE *See page 336.*

REFLECTION

> Did I answer the question Jesus asks: "What do you want
> me to do for you?" (Luke 18:41a).

PRAYER

> In thanksgiving for sharing yourself
> and allowing me to move into your divine mystery,
> I pray, Lord.

CANTICLE Canticle of Zechariah

Morning Prayer

Begin with page 324.

SCRIPTURE Luke 11:3

Give us each day our daily bread.

WORDS OF WISDOM

John Chrysostom tells us, "Regarding the word 'our,' bread is given to us so that not only we might eat but that we recognize others in need, lest anyone say, 'My bread is given to me' instead of understanding that it is ours, given to me, to others through me and to me through others."

Meister Eckhart says, "For not only bread but all things which are necessary for sustaining this present life are given to us with others and because of others and given to others in us. Whosoever does not give to another what belongs to the other, such a one does not eat his own bread but eats the bread of another along with his own. Thus when we justly eat the bread we have received, we certainly eat our bread; but when we eat evilly and with sin the bread we have received, then we are not eating our own bread but the bread of another. For everything which we have unjustly is not really ours."[5]

PRAYER

Our Father....

CANTICLE Canticle of St. Francis

Evening Prayer

Begin with page 325.

SCRIPTURE *See page 338.*

REFLECTION

Do I ever eat another's bread?

PRAYER

Sit in silence and allow the Spirit to answer the reflection question.

CANTICLE Canticle of Mary

Opening Song for Morning Prayer

SALUTATION

Come, glorious morning,
fill the world with new light!

SONG Psalm 67:2-5

May God have pity on us and bless us;
   may he let his face shine upon us.
So may your way be known upon earth;
   among all nations, your salvation.
      May the peoples praise you, O God;
      may all the peoples praise you!

May the nations be glad and exult
   because you rile the peoples in equity;
   the nations on the earth you guide.

*Turn to the page with today's date for the continuation of
Morning Prayer.*

Opening Song for Evening Prayer

SALUTATION

All praise be yours, my Lord, through Sister
Moon and Stars;
In the heavens you have made them, bright,
And precious and fair. (St. Francis)

SONG Psalm 67:5-8

May the nations be glad and exult
because you rule the peoples in equity;
the nations on the earth you guide.
May the peoples praise you, O God;
may all the peoples praise you!

The earth has yielded its fruits;
God, our God has blessed us.
May God bless us,
and may all the ends of the earth fear him!

Turn to the page with today's date for the continuation of Evening Prayer.

Morning Prayer

Begin with page 340.

SCRIPTURE Romans 2:1

Therefore, you are without excuse, every one of you who passes judgment. For by the standard by which you judge another you condemn yourself, since you, the judge, do the very same things.

PUTTING PRAYER INTO PRACTICE

How do you look upon the world? When you meet people whose actions do not fit into your view of what is right or acceptable, do you judge them as wrong or do you believe that people are generally trying to do the best they can? Today, assume that those who irritate you would do better if they knew better. Notice how this attitude affects your relationships with them.

PRAYER

Take from me my self-centeredness,
Spirit of the Universe,
so that I do not see
every act that displeases me
and every word that annoys me
as a deliberate attempt to offend.

CANTICLE Canticle of St. Patrick

Evening Prayer

Begin with page 341.

SCRIPTURE *See page 342.*

REFLECTION

How do I think God will judge me?

PRAYER

Lord, help me
to love the person who inflicts suffering,
to look beyond the action
and see the actor
with eyes of compassion.

CANTICLE Canticle of Zechariah

Morning Prayer

Begin with page 340.

SCRIPTURE Ephesians 1:3-7

Blessed be the God and Father of our Lord Jesus Christ,
who has blessed us in Christ with every spiritual
blessing in the heavens, as he chose us in him, before
the foundation of the world, to be holy and without
blemish before him. In love he destined us for adoption
to himself through Jesus Christ, in accord with the favor
of his will for the praise of the glory of his grace that he
granted us in the beloved.

MEDITATION EXERCISE

Think about what it means to be "chosen before the
foundation of the world" and "adopted in love." Visualize
Christ standing before you and saying, "I have chosen
you."

PRAYER

Help me not to hide from you, God and Savior,
but to walk and live with the assurance
that I am chosen to share in your Kingdom.

CANTICLE Wisdom Canticle

Evening Prayer

Begin with page 341.

SCRIPTURE *See page 344.*

REFLECTION

Down deep in my heart, am I really convinced that I am
chosen?

PRAYER

As the velvet curtain of night falls,
I bask in the knowledge
of your steadfast love, Lord.

CANTICLE Canticle of Judith

Morning Prayer

Begin with page 340.

SCRIPTURE Luke 23:39-43

Now one of the criminals hanging there reviled Jesus,
saying, "Are you not the Messiah? Save yourself and us."
The other, however, rebuking him, said in reply, "Have
you no fear of God, for you are subject to the same
condemnation? And indeed, we have been condemned
justly, for the sentence we received corresponds to our
crimes, but this man has done nothing criminal." Then
he said, "Jesus, remember me when you come into your
kingdom." He replied to him, "Amen, I say to you, today
you will be with me in Paradise."

WORDS OF WISDOM

The Kingdom of God, then, will be a society in which
there will be no prestige and no status, no division of
people into inferior and superior. Everyone will be loved
and respected not because of his education or wealth or
ancestry or authority or rank or virtue or other
achievements, but because he, like everybody else, is a
person. Some will find it very difficult to imagine what
such a life would be like, but the babes who have never
had any of the privileges of status and those who have
not valued it will find it very easy to appreciate the
fulfillment that life in such a society would bring. Those
who could not bear to have beggars, former prostitutes,
servants, women and children treated as their equals,
who could not live without feeling superior to at least

some people, would simply not be at home in God's
kingdom as Jesus understood it. They would want to
exclude themselves from it.[6]

PRAYER

You show us, Brother Jesus,
that if we can love our enemies
and all those people we judge as inferior,
that we are already in Paradise.

CANTICLE Canticle of St. Patrick

Evening Prayer

Begin with page 341.

SCRIPTURE *See page 346.*

REFLECTION Who are the people I don't want to be around?

PRAYER

Thank you, Son of God,
for waking me up
to the realities of Paradise!

CANTICLE Canticle of Zechariah

Morning Prayer

Begin with page 340.

SCRIPTURE Isaiah 32:1-3

See, a king will reign justly
    and princes will rule rightly.
Each of them will be a shelter from the wind,
    a retreat from the rain.
They will be like streams of water in a dry country,
    like the shade of a great rock in a parched land.
The eyes of those who see will not be closed;
    the ears of those who hear will be attentive.

PUTTING PRAYER INTO PRACTICE

It is what you choose to ignore that can control your life.
Today, try to discover one thing that you are ignoring. If
you don't know where to start, notice the things you get
upset over or the areas where you lose control. Explore
the unknown part of yourself with wonder and
acceptance rather than fear and guilt.

PRAYER

Help me to rejoice in the understanding, Lord,
that wholeness or completeness comes from recognizing
both the dark and light sides of my being.

CANTICLE Wisdom Canticle

Evening Prayer

Begin with page 341.

SCRIPTURE *See page 348.*

REFLECTION

Did I discover something about myself today that I had been choosing to ignore?

PRAYER

I celebrate all aspects of my personhood,
even the inferior side of my nature,
and give thanks for life!

CANTICLE Canticle of Mary

Morning Prayer

Begin with page 340.

SCRIPTURE 2 Peter 1:5-7

For this very reason, make every effort to supplement your faith with virtue, virtue with knowledge, knowledge with self-control, self-control with endurance, endurance with devotion, devotion with mutual affection, mutual affection with love.

WORDS OF WISDOM

For what the Lord says is very true: *Where your treasure is, there also will your heart be.* What is a man's treasure but the heaping up of profits and the fruit of his toil. *For whatever a man sows this too will he reap*, and each man's gain matches his toil; and where delight and enjoyment are found, there the heart's desire is attached. Now there are many kinds of wealth and a variety of grounds for rejoicing; every man's treasure is that which he desires. If it is based on earthly ambitions, its acquisition makes men not blessed but wretched. (St. Leo the Great)[7]

PRAYER

Guide my efforts, God,
toward truth and light.
Shield me from shallowness
and the temporary pleasures it brings.

CANTICLE Canticle of Mary

Evening Prayer

Begin with page 341.

SCRIPTURE *See page 350.*

REFLECTION Where do I find my delight and enjoyment?

PRAYER

As I close my prayer,
to you I give thanks, Lord,
for your abiding presence
brings joy and delight.

CANTICLE Canticle of Judith

Morning Prayer

Begin with page 340.

SCRIPTURE Acts 10:9b, 10b-11a, 12-13a, 15b-16a, 19, 20b, 34-35

(Suggestion: Read Acts 10:9-35 in your Bible.)

Peter went up to the roof terrace to pray about noontime...[and] fell into a trance. He saw heaven opened and something resembling a large sheet coming down.... In it were all the earth's four-legged animals and reptiles and the birds of the sky. A voice said to him,... "What God has made clean you are not to profane." This happened three times....

As Peter was pondering the vision, the Spirit said to him, "There are three men here looking for you.... [A]ccompany them without hesitation...."

Then Peter proceeded to speak and said, "In truth I see that God shows no partiality. Rather, in every nation whoever fears him and acts uprightly is acceptable to him."

MEDITATION

Think about how much division and bloodshed has come from the notion that God is partial, preferring one nation or one Church to another.

PRAYER

Divine Spirit,
plunge me into the depths of creation
so that I may find that common root
from which springs the tree of humankind.

CANTICLE Canticle of St. Francis

Evening Prayer

Begin with page 341.

SCRIPTURE Acts 10:35

Rather, in every nation whoever fears him and acts
uprightly is acceptable to him.

REFLECTION

What things cause me revulsion? In what situations is it
difficult for me to see God?

PRAYER

In the midst of confusion and uncertainty,
Lord, you are there,
if only I pause to find you,
in that sacred place within.

CANTICLE Canticle of Judith

Morning Prayer

Begin with page 340.

SCRIPTURE Isaiah 52:11

Depart, depart, come forth from there,
    touch nothing unclean!
Out from there! Purify yourselves,
    you who carry the vessels of the
        LORD.

PUTTING PRAYER INTO PRACTICE

As Ordinary Time draws to a close and Advent begins,
empty yourself by doing an internal housecleaning. So
often we cannot be open to God because we are full of
fear, worries, attachments or guilt. Empty yourself of one
worry today. When the thought begins to gnaw at you,
say a prayer and set it aside.

PRAYER

Lord God, come to my assistance
as I prepare this humble vessel,
both body and soul,
to give birth to the Christ-consciousness.

CANTICLE Canticle of Zechariah

Evening Prayer

Begin with page 341.

SCRIPTURE *See page 354.*

REFLECTION

Make a list of all the clutter you want to clean out of your life. Keep the list in this book or write it in your spiritual journal, if you are keeping one. Read it often.

PRAYER

Maranatha!
We wait in trembling joy
for the advent of your Spirit among us,
Lamb of God!

CANTICLE Canticle of Mary

Morning Prayer

Begin with page 340.

SCRIPTURE Ezekiel 45:1, 7-8

When you apportion the land into inheritances, you shall set apart a sacred tract of land for the LORD, twenty-five thousand cubits long and twenty thousand wide; its whole area shall be sacred.... The prince shall have a section bordering on both sides of the combined sacred tract and City property, extending westward on the western side and eastward on the eastern side, corresponding in length to one of the tribal portions from the western boundary to the eastern boundary of the land. This shall be his property in Israel, so that the princes of Israel will no longer oppress my people, but will leave the land to the house of Israel according to their tribes.

COMMENTARY

Not only does God ask us to apportion some land for the Lord, but also to apportion some land for earthly rulers as well so that they will not oppress the people.

PRAYER

May I extend fairness,
God and Giver of all good things,
in equal measure
to all manner of people
whose paths cross mine.

CANTICLE Canticle of Judith

Evening Prayer

Begin with page 341.

SCRIPTURE *See page 356.*

REFLECTION

In what ways am I compassionate toward my superiors?

PRAYER

Meditate on that special gift that is yours alone—that gift that no one but you can pass on to another.

CANTICLE Canticle of Mary

Morning Prayer

Begin with page 340.

SCRIPTURE Revelation 1:8

"I am the Alpha and the Omega," says the Lord God, "the one who is and who was and who is to come, the almighty."

COMMENTARY

In the philosophy symbolized by the Native American medicine wheel, all of creation, humankind included, is in a constant state of flux or change: waking/sleeping; sowing/reaping; birthing/dying, to name a few. This state of flux moves in an orderly, balanced and rhythmic cycle, like the sun and the seasons.

Autumn is the season of endings: death, loss, illness, burnout, and so on. Winter is the dormant period when, beneath the surface, transformation is occurring. Spring brings new beginnings and birth while summer represents abundance where all things, including plans and dreams, come to fruition.

Each season leads into the next and the soul rotates repeatedly around the positions of this cycle of change, like a car ascending a winding mountain road. With the completion of each cycle, the soul gains a higher, broader perspective, enabling it to complete each new cycle *more conscientiously* than the previous one.

PRAYER

> Before time was, I was,
> and will be again.
> I wait for my homecoming
> with you, eternal God.

CANTICLE Wisdom Canticle

Evening Prayer

Begin with page 341.

SCRIPTURE *See page 358.*

REFLECTION

> Am I able to learn the lessons that each part of my
> journey (rest stops, detours, accelerations) teaches me?

PRAYER

> No matter where my journey takes me,
> whether I'm stretching to grow
> or cowering in fear,
> you are always there to console me,
> Father, Son and Holy Spirit.
>
> Glory be to the Father...

CANTICLE Canticle of Mary

Notes

[1] The excerpt from *Jesus Before Christianity*, by Albert Nolan, copyright ©1992 by Orbis Books, Maryknoll, New York, is reprinted with permission of the publisher.

[2] The excerpt from *Jesus Before Christianity*, by Albert Nolan, copyright ©1992 by Orbis Books, Maryknoll, New York, is reprinted with permission of the publisher.

[3] The excerpt from *Fire From Within*, by Carlos Castañeda, copyright ©1984 by Carlos Castañeda and published by Pocket Books, Simon and Schuster, Inc., is reprinted with permission of the author.

[4] The excerpt from *The Interior Castle*, by St. Teresa of Avila, copyright ©1961 by Andrews, McMeel and Parker, is reprinted with the permission of Andrews, McMeel and Parker.

[5] Fox, Matthew, *Breakthrough: Meister Eckhart's Creation Spirituality* (New York: Image Books, 1980), pp. 449, 500.

[6] The excerpt from *Jesus Before Christianity*, by Albert Nolan, copyright ©1992 by Orbis Books, Maryknoll, New York, is reprinted with permission of the publisher.

[7] The excerpt from *The Liturgy of the Hours*, copyright ©1974, International Committee on English in the Liturgy, Inc. All rights reserved.

December

Opening Song for Morning Prayer

SALUTATION

To you, Yahweh, I give praise
as I greet the new morn!

SONG Psalm 121:1-4

I lift my eyes toward the mountains;
whence shall help come to me?
My help is from the LORD,
who made heaven and earth.

May he not suffer your foot to slip;
may he slumber not who guards you:
Indeed, he neither slumbers nor sleeps,
the guardian of Israel.

Turn to the page with today's date for the continuation of Morning Prayer.

Opening Song for Evening Prayer

SALUTATION

Guard and protect me, Yahweh,
as I wait upon your word
in the quiet of the night.

SONG Psalm 121:5-8

The LORD is your guardian; the LORD is your shade;
  He is beside you at your right hand.
The sun shall not harm you by day,
  nor the moon by night.

The LORD will guard you from all evil;
  he will guard your life.
The LORD will guard your coming and your going,
  both now and forever.

*Turn to the page with today's date for the continuation of
Evening Prayer.*

Morning Prayer

Begin with page 362.

SCRIPTURE Micah 6:8

> You have been told, O man, what is good,
>> and what the LORD requires of you:
> Only to do the right and to love goodness,
>> and to walk humbly with your God.

PUTTING PRAYER INTO PRACTICE

The Advent Season is a time filled with activity. Slow down your actions; avoid scurrying around and shopping frantically. Spend time in stillness and preparation for the gift to come. Advent is a period of waiting—a period of emptying so that you will have space for Christ on Christmas.

PRAYER

> It is not an easy task—to love goodness.
> Sometimes it seems boring or monotonous.
> My grasping heart loves the excitement
> of fleeting pleasures and worldly diversions.
> Help me, Brother Jesus,
> to walk humbly and do right.

CANTICLE Canticle of Zechariah

Evening Prayer

Begin with page 363.

SCRIPTURE *See page 364.*

REFLECTION

Do I sit quietly in prayer and wait on the Lord or am I too busy?

PRAYER

With a warm heart and serene spirit,
I end my prayer and welcome Brother Sleep.

CANTICLE Canticle of St. Francis

Morning Prayer

Begin with page 362.

SCRIPTURE Sirach 5:11-16

Winnow not in every wind,
   and start not off in every direction.
Be consistent in your thoughts;
   steadfast be your words.
Be swift to hear,
   but slow to answer.
If you have the knowledge, answer your neighbor;
   if not, put your hand over your mouth.
Honor and dishonor through talking!
   A man's tongue can be his downfall.
Be not called a detractor,
   use not your tongue for calumny....

WORDS OF WISDOM

Fly the hubbub of men as much as you can, for concern
with worldly affairs is a great hindrance, although they
be entered into with a good intention. For we are soon
tainted by vanity and held captive. Often I have wished
that I had been silent after having been in the company
of men.

But why are we so willing to talk and discourse with one
another, even though we seldom return to silence
without hurt of conscience?

The reason why we are so willing to talk is because by
discoursing together we seek consolation from one

another and we wish to ease our heart, wearied by various thoughts. And we are fond of speaking and thinking of such things that we very much love and desire, or of which we imagine allows us to argue. But alas, it is often in vain, and to no purpose; for this outward consolation is no small hindrance to inward and divine consolation. (Thomas á Kempis)[1]

PRAYER

Restrain my tongue and quiet my thoughts
as I prepare my heart for the Spirit of love.

CANTICLE Wisdom Canticle

Evening Prayer

Begin with page 363.

SCRIPTURE *See page 366.*

REFLECTION

When was I steadfast in my words today?

PRAYER

Thank you, Divine Spirit,
for giving me the presence of mind
to think before I speak.

CANTICLE Canticle of Mary

Morning Prayer

Begin with page 362.

SCRIPTURE Isaiah 49:14-16

> But Zion said, "The LORD has forsaken me;
>   my Lord has forgotten me."
> Can a mother forget her infant,
>   be without tenderness for the child of her womb?
> Even should she forget,
>   I will never forget you.
> See, upon the palms of my hands I have written your
>   name....

REFLECTION

Wrap yourself in God's tender love today. See how dear
you are in the divine Parent's eyes. Turn to your
Father/Mother like a crying child whenever you sense
stress or conflict.

PRAYER

In the midst of my day,
in the turmoil of my emotions,
come to my aid, Father/Mother God,
and remind me that you have carved my name
in the palm of your hand.

CANTICLE Canticle of Judith

Evening Prayer

Begin with page 363.

SCRIPTURE *See page 368.*

REFLECTION

How can I remember to call on the Lord and on my own
higher nature?

PRAYER

By invoking your name, Holy Spirit,
I can bring peace and harmony
to any situation.

CANTICLE Wisdom Canticle

Morning Prayer

Begin with page 362.

SCRIPTURE Isaiah 55:6-9

Seek the LORD while he may be found,
    call him while he is near.
Let the scoundrel forsake his way,
    and the wicked man his thoughts;
Let him turn to the LORD for mercy;
    to our God, who is generous in forgiving.
For my thoughts are not your thoughts,
    nor are your ways my ways, says the LORD.
As high as the heavens are above the earth,
    so high are my ways above your ways
    and my thoughts above your thoughts.

WORDS OF WISDOM

Enter into your mind's inner chamber. Shut out
everything but God and whatever helps you to seek him;
and when you have shut the door, look for him. Speak
now to God and say with your whole heart: *I seek your
face; your face, Lord, I desire.*

Lord, my God, teach my heart where and how to seek
you, where and how to find you. Lord, if you are not here,
where shall I look for you in your absence? Yet if you are
everywhere, why do I not see you when you are present?
But surely you dwell in "light inaccessible." And where is
light inaccessible? How shall I approach light
inaccessible? Or who will lead me and bring me into it
that I may see you there? (St. Anselm)[2]

PRAYER

Lord, my God, teach my heart where and how to seek you.

CANTICLE Wisdom Canticle

Evening Prayer

Begin with page 363.

SCRIPTURE *See page 370.*

REFLECTION Am I doing all that I humanly can to knock down the barriers that keep me from God?

PRAYER

Lord, for the grace
to find your face in all of creation,
I give thanks!

CANTICLE Canticle of St. Francis

Morning Prayer

Begin with page 362.

SCRIPTURE Matthew 7:24-27

Everyone who listens to these words of mine and acts on them will be like a wise man who built his house on rock. The rain fell, the floods came, and the winds blew and buffeted the house. But it did not collapse; it had been set solidly on rock. And everyone who listens to these words of mine but does not act on them will be like a fool who built his house on sand. The rain fell, the floods came, and the winds blew and buffeted the house. And it collapsed and was completely ruined.

PUTTING PRAYER INTO PRACTICE

Consider cutting down on the commercial aspect of Christmas. Spend more time in sacred silence. Think of spiritual things to do with your family, such as going to a concert or singing carols. Let your celebrations of eating and gift-giving take on a spiritual significance.

PRAYER

Help me, Lord, to resist
the commercialization of Christmas.
Television hype and mall decorations
invite me to indulge in consumerism.
Give me the grace to enjoy
only a few nice things
and share my excess with the needy.

CANTICLE Canticle of Zechariah

Evening Prayer

Begin with page 363.

SCRIPTURE *See page 372.*

REFLECTION

How much power does advertising have over me?

PRAYER

For the wisdom and strength
to go beneath the surface
of appearances and activity,
I pray, wise and all-knowing God.

CANTICLE Wisdom Canticle

Morning Prayer

Begin with page 362.

SCRIPTURE John 21:15a, 16b

When they had finished breakfast, Jesus said to Simon Peter, "Simon, son of John, do you love me more than these?" He said to him, "Yes, Lord, you know that I love you." He said to him, "Tend my sheep."

WORDS OF WISDOM

Do you love me? Tend my sheep. Surely this means: "If you love me, your thoughts must focus on taking care of my sheep, not taking care of yourself. You must tend them as mine, not as yours; seek in them my glory, not yours; my sovereign rights, not yours; my gain, not yours. Otherwise, you will find yourself among those who belong to the 'times of peril,' those who are guilty of self-love and the other sins that go with that beginning of evils." (St. Augustine)[3]

COMMENTARY

Nicholas was the bishop of Myra in Lycia (now part of Turkey). He died in the middle of the fourth century and, particularly since the tenth century, has been honored by the whole Christian Church.

PRAYER

In the true spirit of giving,
may I focus on the joys of following God's will
rather than my own.

CANTICLE Canticle of St. Patrick

Evening Prayer

Begin with page 363.

SCRIPTURE *See page 374.*

REFLECTION

What gift can I make to the Lord during this season of
giving? In what way can I tend Christ's sheep?

PRAYER

My joy is complete in you, Lord,
for you are my creator.

CANTICLE Canticle of Mary

Morning Prayer

Begin with page 362.

SCRIPTURE 1 Maccabees 4:52-56

Early in the morning on the twenty-fifth day of the ninth month, that is, the month of Chislev, in the year one hundred forty-eight, they arose and offered sacrifice according to the law on the new altar of holocausts that they had made. On the anniversary of the day on which the Gentiles had defiled it, on that very day it was reconsecrated with songs, harps, flutes, and cymbals. All the people prostrated themselves and adored and praised Heaven, who had given them success.

For eight days they celebrated the dedication of the altar and joyfully offered holocausts and sacrifices of deliverance and praise.

COMMENTARY

Out of the roots of Judaism comes our Christian spirituality. The eight-day Hanukkah celebration comes from the story in Maccabees about that family's fight to win Jews the freedom to practice their beliefs and rededicate the temple. This Jewish holy day celebrates the right of the minority to dissent. The "menorah," an eight- or nine-branched candelabra recalls how the Jews won the right to their own ways of worship.

PUTTING PRAYER INTO PRACTICE

Light a candle today and say a prayer in celebration of tolerance and respect for religious differences.

PRAYER

With the light of this candle, Lord,
I celebrate the diversity and variety
of your creation. Alleluia!

CANTICLE Canticle of Judith

Evening Prayer

Begin with page 363.

SCRIPTURE *See page 376.*

REFLECTION

How do I show my respect for another's religious beliefs?

PRAYER

Blessed is the multitude of your creation, God!

CANTICLE Canticle of St. Francis

Opening Song for Morning Prayer

SALUTATION

Day Star, guide me
as I discern Yahweh's will
and prepare for his presence.

SONG Psalm 24:1-5

The LORD's are the earth and its fullness;
 the world and those who dwell in it.
For he founded it upon the seas
 and established it upon the rivers.

Who can ascend the mountain of the LORD?
 or who may stand in his holy place?
He whose hands are sinless, whose heart is clean,
 who desires not what is vain,
 nor swears deceitfully to his neighbor.
He shall receive a blessing from the LORD,
 a reward from God his savior.

*Turn to the page with today's date for the continuation of
Morning Prayer.*

Opening Song for Evening Prayer

SALUTATION

O Lᴏʀᴅ, I love the house in which you dwell,
the tenting-place of your glory. (Psalm 26:8)

SONG Psalm 16:5-9

O Lᴏʀᴅ, my allotted portion and my cup,
you it is who holds fast my lot.
For me the measuring lines have fallen on pleasant sites;
fair to me indeed is my inheritance.

I bless the Lᴏʀᴅ who counsels me;
even in the night my heart exhorts me.
I set the Lᴏʀᴅ ever before me;
with him at my right hand I shall not be disturbed.
Therefore my heart is glad and my soul rejoices;
my body, too, abides in confidence....

Turn to the page with today's date for the continuation of Evening Prayer.

Morning Prayer

Begin with page 378.

SCRIPTURE Luke 1:30-31, 36-38a

Then the angel said to her, "Do not be afraid, Mary, for you have found favor with God. Behold, you will conceive in your womb and bear a son, and you shall name him Jesus.

"And behold, Elizabeth, your relative, has also conceived a son in her old age, and this is the sixth month for her who was called barren; for nothing will be impossible for God." Mary said, "Behold, I am the handmaid of the Lord. May it be done to me according to your word."

WORDS OF WISDOM

As truly as God is our Father, so truly is God our Mother. Our Father wills, our Mother works, our Good Lord the Holy Spirit confirms.... So, Jesus is our true Mother in nature by our first creation, and He is our true Mother in grace by His taking our created nature....

The Mother's service is nearest, readiest and surest; nearest because it is most natural, readiest because it is most loving, and surest because it is truest. (Julian of Norwich)[4]

PRAYER

Creator God, Father and Mother of the Universe,
Let me unite in myself those qualities of male and female
so that I may be restored to wholeness.

CANTICLE Canticle of St. Francis

Evening Prayer

Begin with page 379.

SCRIPTURE *See page 380.*

REFLECTION

What qualities associated with the opposite sex lie dormant within me, waiting to be developed?

PRAYER

Thank you, wise and loving Lord,
for the balance and rhythm you bestow on creation.

CANTICLE Wisdom Canticle

Morning Prayer

Begin with page 378.

SCRIPTURE Luke 1:13-17

> But the angel said to him, "Do not be afraid, Zechariah, because your prayer has been heard. Your wife Elizabeth will bear you a son, and you shall name him John. And you will have joy and gladness, and many will rejoice at his birth, for he will be great in the sight of [the] Lord. He will drink neither wine nor strong drink. He will be filled with the holy Spirit even from his mother's womb, and he will turn many of the children of Israel to the Lord their God. He will go before him in the spirit and power of Elijah to turn the hearts of fathers toward children and the disobedient to the understanding of the righteous, to prepare a people fit for the Lord."

PUTTING PRAYER INTO PRACTICE

John prepared people for the Lamb of God by asking them to repent. Today choose one way that you can repent as you prepare for Christmas. Make your repentance an act of love such as a daily act of charity or a continuing effort to promote peace. Stick to this task throughout Advent.

PRAYER

Today I rejoice, God,
in anticipation of your gift
to me and to all of humankind—
the Incarnation of Ultimate Love.

CANTICLE Canticle of Zechariah

Evening Prayer

Begin with page 379.

SCRIPTURE *See page 382.*

REFLECTION

What is the importance of Advent to me?

PRAYER

As I prepare to receive
the greatest gift of all,
I sing your praises, Lord,
and proclaim my gratitude!

CANTICLE Canticle of Judith

Morning Prayer

Begin with page 378.

SCRIPTURE Isaiah 11:6-9

Then the wolf shall be a guest of the lamb,
  and the leopard shall lie down with the kid;
The calf and the young lion shall browse together,
  with a little child to guide them.
The cow and the bear shall be neighbors,
  together their young shall rest;
  the lion shall eat hay like the ox.
The baby shall play by the cobra's den,
  and the child lay his hand on the adder's lair.
There shall be no harm or ruin on all my holy mountain;
  for the earth shall be filled with knowledge of the
    LORD,
  as water covers the sea.

MEDITATION EXERCISE

The Kingdom comes when opposites are at peace with
one another. Scripture is full of paradox. The more
spiritually mature the soul, the more comfortable that
soul is with paradox. Meditate on a paradox in your life.
Focus on what the opposing forces are and seek a way
for opposites to "lie down together" in peace.

PRAYER

> Deliver me, Lord, from the need
> to convert, criticize or force another soul
> to do things my way,
> for in your Kingdom there is much variety.

CANTICLE Canticle of St. Francis

Evening Prayer

Begin with page 379.

SCRIPTURE *See page 384.*

REFLECTION

> Is my sense of justice full of love for both the oppressed
> and the oppressor? Or is my sense of justice filled with
> vengeance?

PRAYER

> You, Lord, will give me
> the wisdom and perspective
> to reconcile opposites,
> if only I seek your help!

CANTICLE Wisdom Canticle

Morning Prayer

Begin with page 378.

SCRIPTURE Luke 1:39-45

During those days, Mary set out and traveled to the hill country in haste to a town of Judah, where she entered the house of Zechariah and greeted Elizabeth. When Elizabeth heard Mary's greeting, the infant leaped in her womb, and Elizabeth, filled with the holy Spirit, cried out in a loud voice and said, "Most blessed are you among women, and blessed is the fruit of your womb. And how does this happen to me, that the mother of my Lord should come to me? For at the moment the sound of your greeting reached my ears, the infant in my womb leaped for joy. Blessed are you who believed that what was spoken to you by the Lord would be fulfilled."

MEDITATION EXERCISE

"Blessed are you who believed that what was spoken to you by the Lord would be fulfilled" (Luke 1:45): Meditate on what these words mean to you and how you have incorporated them into your life.

PRAYER

Brother Jesus,
help my unbelief!
Open my eyes, ears and understanding
so that my life will be governed by love
rather than by fear
or a desire for security or status.

CANTICLE Canticle of St. Patrick

Evening Prayer

Begin with page 379.

SCRIPTURE Luke 1:45

Blessed are you who believed that what was spoken to you by the Lord would be fulfilled.

REFLECTION

How have I lived these words today?

PRAYER

Hail, Holy Mary!
Your "fiat" made the Incarnation of Love
a reality.

Hail Mary....

CANTICLE Canticle of Mary

Morning Prayer

Begin with page 378.

SCRIPTURE John 1:6-9, 19-23ab

A man named John was sent from God. He came for testimony, to testify to the light, so that all might believe through him. He was not the light, but came to testify to the light. The true light, which enlightens everyone, was coming into the world.

...And this is the testimony of John. When the Jews from Jerusalem sent priests and Levites [to him] to ask him, "Who are you?" he admitted and did not deny it, but admitted, "I am not the Messiah." So they asked him, "What are you then? Are you Elijah?" And he said, "I am not." "Are you the Prophet?" He answered, "No." So they said to him, "Who are you, so we can give an answer to those who sent us? What do you have to say for yourself?" He said:

"I am 'the voice of one crying out in the desert, "Make straight the way of the Lord....""""

PUTTING PRAYER INTO PRACTICE

Today identify one attitude or habit that is hindering you from "making straight the way of the Lord."

PRAYER

Clear my mind and heart, Lord,
of the dust of distractions
so that I can see clearly "the way."

CANTICLE Canticle of Mary

Evening Prayer

Begin with page 379.

SCRIPTURE John 1:23b

Make straight the way of the Lord.

REFLECTION

In what ways is my light "true," and how do I enlighten others?

PRAYER

The path to you, Lord,
can be full of distracting detours.
Keep me from being sidetracked
into the nooks, crannies and crevices of the road.

CANTICLE Canticle of Zechariah

Morning Prayer

Begin with page 378.

SCRIPTURE Luke 3:16; 7:28a

John answered them all, saying, "I am baptizing you with water, but one mightier than I is coming. I am not worthy to loosen the thongs of his sandals. He will baptize you with the holy Spirit and fire."

"...I tell you, among those born of women, no one is greater than John...."

MEDITATION

Meditate on John's humility. He was, Christ said, the greatest man born to woman, yet with all his gifts and holiness, he remained "small" so that the focus would be on Christ. There was no jealousy in John. Be on guard today against using your gifts and spirituality to bolster yourself rather than another.

PRAYER

Come to my assistance, Lord;
banish my jealous nature!
Help me to encourage and affirm
those around me.

CANTICLE Canticle of St. Patrick

Evening Prayer

Begin with page 379.

SCRIPTURE *See page 390.*

REFLECTION

Was I jealous of another person's gifts today? Did I use my own gifts for selfish reasons?

PRAYER

For the grace and ability
to become aware of the Holy Spirit within me,
I praise and bless your name,
divine Trinity!

CANTICLE Canticle of Mary

Morning Prayer

Begin with page 378.

SCRIPTURE 1 Corinthians 2:9b

"What eye has not seen, and ear has not heard,
and what has not entered the human heart,
what God has prepared for those who love him,"
this God has revealed to us through the Spirit.

WORDS OF WISDOM

The soul cannot enter into these treasures, nor attain
them, unless it first crosses into and enters the thicket of
suffering, enduring interior and exterior labors, and
unless it first receives from God very many blessings in
the intellect and in the senses, and has undergone long
spiritual training....

Would that men might come at last to see it is quite
impossible to reach the thicket of the riches and wisdom
of God except by first entering the thicket of much
suffering, in such a way that the soul finds there its
consolation and desire. The soul that longs for divine
wisdom chooses first, and in truth, to enter the thicket of
the cross. (John of the Cross)[5]

PRAYER

> Grant me the grace
> to embrace the cross,
> which is the gate
> to divine riches and treasure!

CANTICLE Canticle of Zechariah

Evening Prayer

Begin with page 379.

SCRIPTURE *See page 392.*

REFLECTION

> How often do I seek the fruit of the harvest without being
> willing to toil in the fields?

PRAYER

> For the promise and the vision
> of your divine treasure,
> I thank you, eternal God.

CANTICLE Wisdom Canticle

Opening Song for Morning Prayer

SALUTATION

> Sing out, O heavens, and rejoice, O earth,
> > break forth into song, you mountains.
> For the LORD comforts his people
> > and shows mercy to his afflicted. (Isaiah 49:13)

SONG Psalm 85:1-8

> You have favored, O LORD, your land;
> > you have restored the well-being of Jacob.
> You have forgiven the guilt of your people;
> > you have covered all their sins.
> You have withdrawn all your rage;
> > you have revoked your burning anger.
> Restore us, O God, our savior,
> > and abandon your displeasure against us.
> Will you be ever angry with us,
> > prolonging your anger to all generations?
> Will you not instead give us life;
> > and shall not your people rejoice in you?
> Show us, O LORD, your kindness,
> and grant us your salvation.

*Turn to the page with today's date for the continuation of
Morning Prayer.*

Opening Song for Evening Prayer

SALUTATION

Though the mountains leave their place
and the hills be shaken,
My love shall never leave you
nor my covenant of peace be shaken,
says the LORD, who has mercy on you. (Isaiah 54:10)

SONG Psalm 85:9-12

I will hear what God proclaims;
the LORD—for he proclaims peace.
To his people, and to his faithful ones,
and to those who put in him their hope.
Near indeed is his salvation for those who fear him,
glory dwelling in our land.
Kindness and truth shall meet;
justice and peace shall kiss.
Truth shall spring out of the earth,
and justice shall look down from heaven.

Turn to the page with today's date for the continuation of Evening Prayer.

Morning Prayer

Begin with page 394.

SCRIPTURE Matthew 11:12-15

From the days of John the Baptist until now, the
kingdom of heaven suffers violence, and the violent are
taking it by force. All the prophets and the law
prophesied up to the time of John. And if you are willing
to accept it, he is Elijah, the one who is to come.
Whoever has ears ought to hear.

COMMENTARY

Pope John Paul II's encyclical *On Social Concerns*
suggests that it is society's attitude toward profit and
power that inhibits or prohibits the building of the
Kingdom of God here on earth. While money and power
are not bad in themselves, if used unselfishly, many
times they are used to oppress and control. People of
wealth and power seek to force their way into the
Kingdom by buying love, happiness or whatever it is
they perceive will bring them fulfillment.

PRAYER

Wise and gentle Spirit divine,
help me to understand
that in my need for power and profit
I often create environments that destroy peace.

CANTICLE Canticle of St. Patrick

Evening Prayer

Begin with page 395.

SCRIPTURE *See page 396.*

REFLECTION

Did I notice at least one time today when my pride or my
need for power created conflict within a relationship?

PRAYER

Thank you for the gift of pride
and a healthy ego, Lord.
May I share them in your Kingdom
rather than store them
in my own little treasury.

CANTICLE Canticle of Zechariah

Morning Prayer

Begin with page 394.

SCRIPTURE Micah 4:2-3

Many nations shall come, and say,
"Come, let us climb the mount of the LORD,
    to the house of the God of Jacob.
That he may instruct us in his ways,
    that we may walk in his paths."
For from Zion shall go forth instruction,
    and the word of the LORD from Jerusalem.
He shall judge between many peoples
    and impose terms on strong and distant nations;
They shall beat their swords into plowshares,
    and their spears into pruning hooks;
One nation shall not raise the sword against another,
    nor shall they train for war again.

PUTTING PRAYER INTO PRACTICE

Practice letting down your shield, your guard, and
allowing your vulnerable side to be exposed. It takes the
trust and innocence of a child to do this because you
must cease to perceive the world and other creatures as
your enemy.

PRAYER

Today I will try to be vulnerable, Lord,
to give birth to the holy child within me.
For it is only when I am willing to drop my defenses
that I am able to beat my swords into plowshares.

CANTICLE Canticle of St. Patrick

Evening Prayer

Begin with page 395.

SCRIPTURE *See page 398.*

REFLECTION

In what ways can I be more open and trusting?

PRAYER

I pray, eternal God,
for that holy child within me
that is struggling toward birth
just as the child Jesus did years ago.

CANTICLE Canticle of Mary

Morning Prayer

Begin with page 394.

SCRIPTURE Isaiah 61:1-2

> The spirit of the Lord God is upon me,
>   because the LORD has anointed me;
> He has sent me to bring glad tidings to the lowly,
>   to heal the brokenhearted,
> To proclaim liberty to captives
>   and release to the prisoners,
> To announce a year of favor from the LORD
>   and a day of vindication by our God,
>   to comfort all who mourn....

PUTTING PRAYER INTO PRACTICE

We are all captives to our fears, addictions and passions. Liberate yourself a little today by discovering one need or attachment that you feel you could not live without. Look for such hidden habits as compulsive cleaning or the need to set someone straight.

PRAYER

> Give me the wisdom,
> wise and loving God,
> to discover my own bondage.

CANTICLE Wisdom Canticle

Evening Prayer

Begin with page 395.

SCRIPTURE *See page 400.*

REFLECTION

Did I discover a passion, habit or urge today that I was
unaware of before?

ANTIPHON*

O Wisdom, O holy Word of God, you govern all creation
with your strong yet tender care. Come and show your
people the way to salvation.[6]

CANTICLE Canticle of Zechariah

---

* These ancient prayers, called the "O Antiphons" because they all begin
with "O," are part of the Liturgy of the Hours on the seven days before
Christmas.

Morning Prayer

Begin with page 394.

SCRIPTURE Matthew 3:1-2; 4-8

In those days John the Baptist appeared, preaching in the desert of Judea [and] saying, "Repent, for the kingdom of heaven is at hand!"

...John wore clothing made of camel's hair and had a leather belt around his waist. His food was locusts and wild honey. At that time Jerusalem, all Judea, and the whole region around the Jordan were going out to him and were being baptized by him in the Jordan River as they acknowledged their sins.

When he saw many of the Pharisees and Sadducees coming to his baptisms, he said to them, "You brood of vipers! Who warned you to flee from the coming wrath? Produce good fruit as evidence of your repentance."

PUTTING PRAYER INTO PRACTICE

What is good fruit? Good fruit is the harvest of love and unselfishness. Isn't it comforting to realize that as a human being you have only one need—the need to love? You can fulfill that need in a concentration camp, at home with your family, waiting in line at the grocery store, at work. Remember that the more you love and meet your own need to love, the more fulfilling a life you will lead.

PRAYER

God, Love,
you made me in your likeness.
You fill me with your love;
let it spill over wherever I walk.

CANTICLE Canticle of Mary

Evening Prayer

Begin with page 395.

SCRIPTURE *See page 402.*

REFLECTION

When I have a tendency to get depressed or feel sorry
for myself, I will remember that I have the choice to
continue to indulge that mood or to reach out and fulfill
my need to love.

ANTIPHON

O sacred Lord of ancient Israel, who showed yourself to
Moses in the burning bush, who gave him the holy law
on Sinai mountain: come stretch out your mighty hand to
set us free.[7]

CANTICLE Canticle of Zechariah

Morning Prayer

Begin with page 394.

SCRIPTURE John 5:35

[John the Baptist] was a burning and shining lamp, and for a while you were content to rejoice in his light.

MEDITATION

Think about the person in your life who is a bright light for you. How does that person move and talk and react with others? Chances are, this person is not hurried by a million projects to accomplish but is willing to take time with you. This willingness stems from love or concern. Like John, that person is probably not distracted by appearances or possessions. Meditate on how you can become a shining light to someone else.

PRAYER

Clear out the cobwebs in my thinking, Lord;
release me from my attachments to things.
Cleanse my heart, Christ my Savior,
so that I may become transparent
and reflect your light within me.

CANTICLE Canticle of St. Patrick

Evening Prayer

Begin with page 395.

SCRIPTURE *See page 404.*

REFLECTION

What is blocking or dimming Christ's light within me?

ANTIPHON

O Flower of Jesse's stem, you have been raised up as a sign for all peoples; kings stand silent in your presence; nations bow down in worship before you. Come, let nothing keep you from coming to our aid.[8]

CANTICLE Canticle of Judith

Morning Prayer

Begin with page 394.

SCRIPTURE Matthew 11:28-30

Come to me, all you who labor and are burdened, and I will give you rest. Take my yoke upon you and learn from me, for I am meek and humble of heart; and you will find rest for yourselves. For my yoke is easy, and my burden light.

WORDS OF WISDOM

The essence of spirituality may be knowing how to allow things to happen. (Author unknown)

PUTTING PRAYER INTO PRACTICE

It is not uncommon for the disciples of Christ to get caught up in workaholism or what the psychologists refer to as the Messiah complex. No matter how dedicated or spiritual the individual, one must take the time to renew one's inner strength. Human beings have human limits, and it takes a certain amount of humility to admit this. If you are moving in harmony with the divine plan, there is no need to rush or force things. The more you are in sync with God's plan, the more naturally and easily this divine plan will unfold around you.

PRAYER

Thank you, God,
for the wisdom you instill in me.

Even my body tells me when I am overburdened.
In hope and anticipation
that I will find my limits and niche
within your master plan,
I pray to you, divine Architect!

CANTICLE Canticle of Mary

Evening Prayer

Begin with page 395.

SCRIPTURE *See page 406.*

REFLECTION

Do I overschedule myself to feel more important?

ANTIPHON

O Key of David, O royal Power of Israel controlling at
your will the gate of heaven: come, break down the
prison walls of death for those who dwell in darkness and
the shadow of death; and lead your captive people into
freedom.[9]

CANTICLE Wisdom Canticle

Morning Prayer

Begin with page 394.

SCRIPTURE John 1:1-5

In the beginning was the Word
and the Word was with God,
and the Word was God.
He was in the beginning with God.
All things came to be through him,
and without him nothing came to be.
What came to be through him was life,
and this life was the light of the human race;
the light shines in the darkness,
and the darkness has not overcome it.

PUTTING PRAYER INTO PRACTICE

On this, the shortest day of the year, the winter solstice,
it is good to reflect on the darkness in our lives and how
Christ's strength within us can overcome the darkness.
If you are living in a state of darkness or depression now,
do not let your present weakness direct your actions.
Rather, let go of your sadness and open yourself up to
the light of God's grace.

PRAYER

Overcome my darkness with your light, Divine
Incarnation!

CANTICLE Canticle of Zechariah

Evening Prayer

Begin with page 395.

SCRIPTURE *See page 408.*

REFLECTION

Did I make an effort today to let go of any sadness or darkness that had overtaken me?

ANTIPHON

O Radiant Dawn, splendor of eternal light, sun of justice: come, shine on those who dwell in darkness and the shadow of death.[10]

CANTICLE Canticle of St. Francis

Opening Song for Morning Prayer

SALUTATION

Come Christ, King of Love,
make your home in my heart.
I rejoice each morning
in the knowledge of your presence.

SONG Psalm 96:1-7

Sing to the LORD a new song;
    sing to the LORD, all you lands!
Sing to the LORD, bless his name;
    announce his salvation, day after day.
Tell his glory among the nations;
    among all people, his wondrous deeds.

For great is the LORD and highly to be praised;
    awesome is he, beyond all gods.
For all the gods of the nations are things of nought,
    but the LORD made the heavens.
Splendor and majesty go before him;
    praise and grandeur are in his sanctuary.

Give to the LORD, you families of nations,
    give to the LORD glory and praise....

Turn to the page with today's date for the continuation of Morning Prayer.

Opening Song for Evening Prayer

SALUTATION

At night I find rest, Yahweh;
my eyes find rest
with words of praise for you on my lips.

SONG Psalm 96:8b-13

Bring gifts, and enter his courts;
worship the LORD in holy attire.
Tremble before him, all the earth;
say among the nations: The LORD is king.
He has made the world firm, not to be moved;
he governs the peoples with equity.

Let the heavens be glad and the earth rejoice;
let the sea and what fills it resound;
let the plains be joyful and all that is in them!
Then shall all the trees of the forest exult
before the LORD, for he comes;
for he comes to rule the earth.
He shall rule the world with justice
and the peoples with his constancy.

Turn to the page with today's date for the continuation of Evening Prayer.

Morning Prayer

Begin with page 410.

SCRIPTURE Luke 1:46b-55

My soul proclaims the greatness of the Lord;
　　my spirit rejoices in God my Savior.
For he has looked upon his handmaid's lowliness:
　　behold, from now on will all ages call me blessed.
The Mighty One has done great things for me,
　　and holy is his name.
His mercy is from age to age
　　to those who fear him.
He has shown might with his arm,
　　dispersed the arrogant of mind and heart.
He has thrown down the rulers from their thrones,
　　but lifted up the lowly.
The hungry he has filled with good things;
　　the rich he has sent away empty.
He has helped Israel his servant,
　　remembering his mercy,
according to his promise to our fathers,
　　to Abraham and to his descendants forever.

REFLECTION

How many great things has the Lord done for me and
how often do I take them for granted?

PRAYER

> O Spirit of Love, Divine Energy,
> by your Incarnation
> you sow within me
> the seeds of unconditional love.

CANTICLE Canticle of Zechariah

Evening Prayer

Begin with page 411.

SCRIPTURE *See page 412.*

REFLECTION

> How many more great things is the Lord waiting to do
> for me if only I say, "Let it be done according to thy will"?

ANTIPHON

> O King of all the nations, the only joy of every human
> heart; O Keystone of the mighty arch of [humanity],
> come and save the creatures you fashioned from dust.[11]

CANTICLE Canticle of St. Francis

Morning Prayer

Begin with page 410.

SCRIPTURE Malachi 3:1-2a

Lo, I am sending my messenger
  to prepare the way before me;
And suddenly there will come to the temple
  the LORD whom you seek,
And the messenger of the covenant whom you desire.
Yes, he is coming, says the LORD of hosts.
But who will endure the day of his coming?
  And who can stand when he appears?

PUTTING PRAYER INTO PRACTICE

See the ways today in which God speaks to you. Discover
who his messengers are.

PRAYER

In the person I avoid,
in the embarrassing situation,
in my secret fears:
you are there, Christ,
to comfort and confront me.

CANTICLE Canticle of St. Patrick

Evening Prayer

Begin with page 411.

SCRIPTURE *See page 414.*

REFLECTION

Did the Christ in me greet the Christ in others today?

ANTIPHON

O Emmanuel, king and lawgiver, desire of the nations, Savior of all people, come and set us free, Lord our God.[12]

CANTICLE Canticle of Judith

Morning Prayer

Begin with page 410.

SCRIPTURE Luke 2:8-18

Now there were shepherds in that region living in the fields and keeping the night watch over their flock. The angel of the Lord appeared to them and the glory of the Lord shone around them, and they were struck with great fear. The angel said to them, "Do not be afraid; for behold, I proclaim to you good news of great joy that will be for all the people. For today in the city of David a savior has been born for you who is Messiah and Lord. And this will be a sign for you: you will find an infant wrapped in swaddling clothes and lying in a manger." And suddenly there was a multitude of the heavenly host with the angel, praising God and saying:

Glory to God in the highest and on earth peace to those on whom his favor rests.

PUTTING PRAYER INTO PRACTICE

Carry the angels' message of peace everywhere you go today.

PRAYER

> There's a song in the air!
> There's a star in the sky!
> There's a mother's deep prayer
>   And a Baby's low cry!
> And the star rains its fire where the Beautiful sing,
> For the manger at Bethlehem cradles a King.

(Josiah Gilbert Holland, "A Christmas Carol")

CANTICLE Canticle of Zechariah

Evening Prayer

Begin with page 411.

SCRIPTURE *See page 416.*

REFLECTION

Imagine the trust, patience and stamina of Mary and Joseph as they let God's will unfold in their lives on the first Christmas.

PRAYER AND MEDITATION

Read again the prayer poem above and meditate, imagining the radiance of Christ entering your being.

CANTICLE Canticle of Mary

Morning Prayer

Begin with page 410.

SCRIPTURE Luke 2:16-19

So [the shepherds] went in haste and found Mary and Joseph, and the infant lying in the manger. When they saw this, they made known the message that had been told them about this child. All who heard it were amazed by what had been told them by the shepherds. And Mary kept all these things, reflecting upon them in her heart.

PUTTING PRAYER INTO PRACTICE

Allow the spirit of love to reign at your Christmas table today. As you get together with family and friends, make no judgments and put all grudges aside. Celebrate what you have in common! Accept all just as they are.

PRAYER

O Lamb of God,
you come to teach me love's priorities,
yet I allow appearances to block
the beauty of your beatitudes.

CANTICLE Canticle of St. Patrick

Evening Prayer

Begin with page 411.

SCRIPTURE *See page 418.*

REFLECTION

> *Emmanuel* means "God is with us." Do I live as though I believe these words?

PRAYER

> You became human
> so that I can become divine.
> I love you,
> Eternal God and Living Son!

CANTICLE Canticle of Zechariah

Morning Prayer

Begin with page 410.

SCRIPTURE John 1:10-11

He was in the world,
  and the world came to be through him,
  but the world did not know him.
He came to what was his own,
  but his own people did not accept him.

WORDS OF WISDOM

A little boy was heartbroken to find his pet turtle lying on its back, lifeless and still, beside the pond.

His father did his best to console him: "Don't cry, son. We'll arrange a lovely funeral for Mr. Turtle. We'll make him a little coffin all lined in silk and get the undertaker to make a headstone for his grave, with Mr. Turtle's name carved on it. Then we'll have fresh flowers placed on the grave each day and make a little picket fence to go all around it."

The little boy dried his eyes and became enthusiastic about the project. When all was ready the cortege was formed—father, mother, maid and child chief mourner—and began to move solemnly toward the pond to bring in the body. But the body had vanished.

Suddenly they spied Mr. Turtle emerging from the depths of the pond and swimming around merrily. The little boy stared at his friend in bitter disappointment, then said, "Let's kill him." (Anthony de Mello, S.J.)[13]

PRAYER

> Help me, Lamb of God,
> to understand the mystery of love.

CANTICLE Canticle of Zechariah

Evening Prayer

Begin with page 411.

SCRIPTURE *See page 420.*

REFLECTION

> Anthony de Mello says, "It isn't really you I care about
> but the thrill I get from loving you." How many of your
> loves does this describe?

PRAYER

> For the curiosity to ask, "What is love?"
> and the courage to find out,
> I thank you, Blessed Trinity!

CANTICLE Canticle of St. Francis

Morning Prayer

Begin with page 410.

SCRIPTURE Matthew 2:1-2; 9-11ab

When Jesus was born in Bethlehem of Judea, in the days of King Herod, behold, magi from the east arrived in Jerusalem, saying, "Where is the newborn King of the Jews? We saw his star at its rising and have come to do him homage."

...After their audience with the king they set out. And behold, the star that they had seen at its rising preceded them, until it came and stopped over the place where the child was. They were overwhelmed at seeing the star, and on entering the house they saw the child with Mary his mother. They prostrated themselves and did him homage.

MEDITATION

Silently meditate on the significance of the visit of the magi to the Christ child.

PRAYER

O sanctifying star!
Enter, ablaze, into my soul.
Set fire to my creativity and compassion.
Cleanse from my heart's hearth,
the ashes of indifference.
Abide in me, Lord of Love!

CANTICLE Wisdom Canticle

Evening Prayer

Begin with page 411.

SCRIPTURE *See page 422.*

REFLECTION

How are we stars for each other?

PRAYER

May the star of Christmas shine upon us and reflect its light to all that we touch!

CANTICLE Canticle of St. Francis

Morning Prayer

Begin with page 410.

SCRIPTURE Matthew 8:5-10

When Jesus entered Capernaum, a centurion approached him and appealed to him, saying, "Lord, my servant is lying at home paralyzed, suffering dreadfully." He said to him, "I will come and cure him." The centurion said in reply, "Lord, I am not worthy to have you enter under my roof; only say the word and my servant will be healed. For I too am a person subject to authority, with soldiers subject to me. And I say to one, 'Go,' and he goes; and to another, 'Come here,' and he comes; and to my slave, 'Do this,' and he does it." When Jesus heard this, he was amazed and said to those following him, "Amen, I say to you, in no one in Israel have I found such faith."

PUTTING PRAYER INTO PRACTICE

Christ will enter under your roof and heal you if you allow him in. Are you willing to subject your emotions to healing? Or do you allow them to be master over you? Today, when you feel your emotions taking control, take a deep breath and pray: "May Christ's strength restore me to harmony." See a deeper level within yourself where you will find Christ's strength.

PRAYER

May Christ's strength restore me to harmony
when sadness, depression or anger engulf me.

CANTICLE Canticle of Mary

Evening Prayer

Begin with page 411.

SCRIPTURE *See page 424.*

REFLECTION

At what times today did I overcome negativity and restore harmony to my being by calling on Christ's strength?

PRAYER

For the power and grace
to master my emotions,
I thank you, Brother Jesus.

CANTICLE Wisdom Canticle

Morning Prayer

Begin with page 410.

SCRIPTURE Luke 6:27b-28, 35b

[L]ove your enemies, do good to those who hate you, bless those who curse you, pray for those who mistreat you.... [L]ove your enemies and do good to them, and lend expecting nothing back; then your reward will be great and you will be children of the Most High, for he himself is kind to the ungrateful and the wicked.

MEDITATION

The miracle of the Christ Child is that love interrupts your life and makes it miraculous. It is normal to hate your enemies, not love them. It is normal for the rich to hoard their goods and enjoy them selfishly. It is miraculous for the rich to renounce their goods. It happens because of their love for something greater than possessions. Love turns your normal or natural values upside down. Love of God brings the miraculous into your life.

PRAYER

Lamb of God,
help me to escape
the boundaries of the mind,
and to cross the line
from natural to supernatural,
stepping into the miracle of life!

CANTICLE Canticle of St. Patrick

Evening Prayer

Begin with page 411.

SCRIPTURE *See page 426.*

REFLECTION

Am I blocking the Christ-power within me?

PRAYER

You give me your essence
for my bread of life.
You die so that I may live.
What can I do, my God,
in the face of such love?

CANTICLE Canticle of Zechariah

Morning Prayer

Begin with page 410.

SCRIPTURE Exodus 3:14a

God replied, "I am who am."

COMMENTARY

As we approach the end of a year and celebrate the death of the old and the birth of the new, it is good to remember that our spirit transcends time. The more we live in the spirit, the more we live beyond or outside of death because the spirit does not die. God is being, not doing. To live, more and more, in a conscious state of "being" is to live in eternity here and now.

PUTTING PRAYER INTO PRACTICE

You are who you are, not what you do. Today, be aware of your "doing" and gradually, through the year, see if your doing can become more and more a reflection of your being.

If your doing is limited by a physical disability, you have more opportunity than others to become aware of your "being." Are you cheerful, pleasant and patient with those around you or are you demanding?

PRAYER

> God of Consciousness,
> may I dip beneath the frothy waves
> to the whirling vortex
> where communion occurs.
> Give me the courage,
> Master of the Deep,
> to take the dive!

CANTICLE Canticle of Mary

Evening Prayer

Begin with page 411.

SCRIPTURE *See page 428.*

REFLECTION Do I cling to the surface of living?

PRAYER

> Spirit of mystery and substance,
> you invite me to dance
> and discover my being.
> For your graceful lead,
> I give thanks and praise!

CANTICLE Canticle of Judith

Morning Prayer

Begin with page 410.

SCRIPTURE 1 John 1:1-2

What was from the beginning,
what we have heard,
what we have seen with our eyes,
what we looked upon
and touched with our hands
concerns the Word of life—
for the life was made visible;
we have seen it and testify to it
and proclaim to you the eternal life
that was with the Father and was made visible to us....

PUTTING PRAYER INTO PRACTICE

The more aware we are of time, the more aware we are of limits. To think in terms of time is to think in terms of the temporal life. It is only when we are willing to lose ourselves in the ecstasy of the moment that we become eternal. Lose yourself in something today. Allow time to swallow you up.

PRAYER

> Eternal Father,
> distract me from Father Time.
> Let me be dazzled by the moment,
> attentive to what is happening now,
> so that I may transcend time
> and live in the experience
> that eternity is now.

CANTICLE Wisdom Canticle

Evening Prayer

Begin with page 411.

SCRIPTURE *See page 430.*

REFLECTION

> How often was I present to the moment today?

PRAYER

> For the gift of time,
> which helps me set limits,
> and the gift of eternity,
> which leads me to fathom the unfathomable,
> I give thanks.

CANTICLE Canticle of Judith

Notes

[1] From *The Imitation of Christ*.

[2] The excerpt from *The Liturgy of the Hours*, ©1975, International Committee on English in the Liturgy, Inc. All rights reserved.

[3] Excerpt from *The Liturgy of the Hours*, ©1975, International Committee on English in the Liturgy, Inc. All rights reserved.

[4] The excerpt from *Showings*, by Julian of Norwich, copyright ©1978 by Paulist Press, is reprinted with permission of the publisher, Paulist Press.

[5] The excerpt from *The Liturgy of the Hours*, ©1975, International Committee on English in the Liturgy, Inc. All rights reserved.

[6] The excerpt from *The Liturgy of the Hours*, ©1975, International Committee on English in the Liturgy, Inc. All rights reserved.

[7] The excerpt from *The Liturgy of the Hours*, ©1975, International Committee on English in the Liturgy, Inc. All rights reserved.

[8] The excerpt from *The Liturgy of the Hours* ©1975, International Committee on English in the Liturgy, Inc. All rights reserved.

[9] The excerpt from *The Liturgy of the Hours*, ©1975, International Committee on English in the Liturgy, Inc. All rights reserved.

[10] The excerpt from *The Liturgy of the Hours*, ©1975, International Committee on English in the Liturgy, Inc. All rights reserved.

[11] The excerpt from *The Liturgy of the Hours*, ©1975, International Committee on English in the Liturgy, Inc. All rights reserved.

[12] The excerpt from *The Liturgy of the Hours*, ©1975, International Committee on English in the Liturgy, Inc. All rights reserved.

[13] The excerpt from *The Prayer of the Frog*, by Anthony de Mello, S.J., copyright ©1988 by Gujarat Sahitta Prakash, Anand, India, is reprinted by permission of the publisher.